The Hidden Work

The Hidden Work

What Separates Top Performers From Underachievers

Weston Kieschnick

ConnectEDD Publishing
Hanover, Pennsylvania

Copyright © 2025 by Weston Kieschnick

All rights reserved. No part of this publication may be reproduced, distributed, or transmitted in any form or by any means, including photocopying, recording, or other electronic or mechanical methods, without the prior written permission of the publisher, except in the case of brief quotations embodied in critical reviews and certain other noncommercial uses permitted by copyright law. For permission requests, contact the publisher at: info@connecteddpublishing.com

This publication is available at discount pricing when purchased in quantity for educational purposes, promotions, or fundraisers. For inquiries and details, contact the publisher at: info@connecteddpublishing.com

Published by ConnectEDD Publishing LLC
Hanover, PA
www.connecteddpublishing.com

Cover Design: Kheila Casas

The Hidden Work —1st ed. Paperback
ISBN   979-8-9933700-1-9

Praise for *The Hidden Work*

The Hidden Work cuts straight to the truth. It's quick, relatable, and absolutely vital for anyone who wants to separate from the pack. Remember—life is a daily selection process, and it's the hidden work that decides who stands out.

–Matt Bissonnette | aka Mark Owen New York Times Best-Selling Author of *No Easy Day* Seal Team 6

The Hidden Work is a masterclass in mindset and performance. Kieschnick strips away the noise and gets to the truth behind what separates those who talk about excellence from *those who actually live it*. With authenticity, humor, and hard-won wisdom, he reminds us that success isn't built in public; it's forged in the unseen effort that no one applauds. This book will challenge you, inspire you, and quite possibly change the way you lead, teach, and live!

–Thomas C. Murray | Best-Selling Author Director of Innovation, *Future* Ready Schools

Weston Kieschnick's *The Hidden Work* combines research, reflection, and real life. It is not about grinding harder; it is about leading yourself with honesty and purpose. Kieschnick reveals the patterns that drain performance, such as blame, excuses, self-deception, and quitting, and shows how to replace them with habits that build strength: ownership, problem solving, truth, and grit.

What sets this book apart is its subtext. It isn't just about self-discipline; it's about modeling the kind of accountability that builds psychological safety in teams. Leaders who read this will find both a mirror and a method.

This book doesn't ask you to be perfect. It asks you to be responsible for what you create in yourself, in others, and in the cultures you lead.

–Amy Dujon | Arc Network, Vice-President Educator, Author, Speaker

We are capable of more than we can even imagine, but our most significant obstacle to achieving it is often ourselves. In *The Hidden Work*, author Weston Kieschnick helps us identify the challenges we put in our own way, and shows us how to move beyond them with purpose and courage. Through powerful storytelling, practical strategies, heartfelt inspiration, and a needed kick in the pants, Weston reminds us that the most transformative work we'll ever do happens within.

–Allyson Apsey | Best-Selling Author, National Keynote Speaker, and Director of Client Relations at *Creative Leadership Solutions*

This isn't just a book about performance; it's a blueprint for dismantling the mental barriers that keep you stuck. Kieschnick leverages deep psychological and evolutionary insights to expose the four insidious pitfalls that include blame, excuses, self-deception, and giving up. For any leader, educator, or individual committed to high standards, this book is essential: it doesn't just ask you to aim higher, it equips you with the conscious, actionable patterns: ownership, solutions, self-confrontation, and grit—to actually get there. *The Hidden Work* is a powerful, must-read guide to building a culture of excellence, starting first with yourself.

–Eric Sheninger | Author, Award-Winning Principal, Speaker

This book is a gut check for anyone serious about growth (and what may be holding you back)! *The Hidden Work* doesn't just teach performance...it reveals the inner disciplines, mental resets, and honest reflection required to own it. If you want to understand what really fuels success, this is where YOU start!

–LaVonna Roth | Keynote Speaker & Chief Illuminator *Ignite Your S.H.I.N.E.*

There is undeniable truth in Weston Kieschnick's words: it is the unseen effort—the work that some refuse to do, few recognize, and almost none fully understand—that distinguishes top performers from underachievers. His honest and personal approach, coupled with his emphasis on taking ownership of our performance, rejecting excuses and blame, and persevering through challenges, will resonate with leaders in any field.

–Laurie Barron | Superintendent, Evergreen (MT) School District

Practical Brilliance. Weston masterfully blends story, strategy, and soul—offering tangible tools and gentle reminders that the work is hard, and always worth it.

–Dr. Jessica Cabeen | Award Winning Principal, Speaker, and Author

Weston Kieschnick's *The Hidden Work* is a masterclass in what truly separates high performers from those who stall—and it's not talent, luck, or timing. With powerful psychology and candid storytelling, Kieschnick unpacks how blame, excuses, and self-deception quietly derail our growth, and how ownership, honesty, and grit transform it. This is a book for leaders and educators who understand that excellence starts within and is built through consistent, uncomfortable practice. Inspiring, actionable, and humbling in all the right ways, *The Hidden Work* challenges every reader to show up differently tomorrow.

–Joe Sanfelippo | Retired Superintendent, Author, Speaker

Dedication

To my family: Molly, Everett, and Charlotte. You teach me that the most sacred work is the kind no audience ever sees. You remind me daily that the unseen effort is the truest kind of love.

And to every person who has ever wondered if they are enough, who has wrestled with doubt in the quiet hours, who has fought battles no one else noticed—this book is for you. Your hidden work is not wasted. It is the quiet architecture of your greatness.

Table of Contents

Introduction: *Performance: It's an Inside Job*. 1

Chapter 1: *Choice: The Line Between Low and Top Performance* 7

Chapter 2: *Ownership: The Antidote to Blame* 23
    The Psychology Behind Blame 26
    Ownership: A Pattern of Top Performance 30

Chapter 3: *Solutions: Escaping the Excuse Trap* 37
    Excuses: The Quiet Exit from the Arena 39
    The Psychology Behind Excuses. 42
    From Excuses to Solutions 44
    Reasons are Real. Excuses are Optional. Motion
        is Mandatory. 47
    Becoming a Problem Solver 48

Chapter 4: *Self-Confrontation: Self-Deceptions that Hold Us Back* 51
    Two Sides of Self-Deception, Same Result. 54
    The Psychology of Self-Deception. 55
    Confronting the Cold, Hard Truth 57
    Ways to Self-Confront…With Care 62
    Let's Take a Page from Goggins 63

Chapter 5: *Grit: Resisting the Pull to Give Up* 65
    What It Means to Give Up 66
    The Psychology of Giving Up 67
    Failing the Way to Top Performance 70
    The Power of Grit 72
    How to Build Grit 74
    When Others Tell Us to Give Up 75
    Grit Pays Us Back in Spades 77

Chapter 6: *Culture: Building an Ecosystem of Excellence* 81
    The Five Steps to Creating a Culture of Top Performance 84

Afterword: *You Hold the Power* 91

References 95

Acknowledgements 99

About the Author 101

More from ConnectEDD Publishing 103

INTRODUCTION

Performance: It's an Inside Job

The line between success and failure isn't just drawn on your heart. It's carved in your habits.

Since 2012, I've been coaching football at a local high school in Denver. My obsession with peak performance has led me to study every strategy and tactic I can find—not just to raise my own game, but to help those I coach reach new levels, too. One of the most powerful tools I've found as a football coach is simple: I train with the boys. On the field, I'm on the sidelines coaching. But in the gym, I'm on the floor with them—sweating, spotting, pushing through reps.

There's a principle behind this practice. I'll never ask the kids to do something I wouldn't do myself. It's how I model commitment. It's how I show them what it looks like to work, improve, show up with purpose. It's a lesson I've learned over time about performance: Top performers never demand what they're not willing to demonstrate.

It's also connection. We partner up for every workout, which means I get quality time with each kid. I hold them accountable. They hold me accountable. And—call it hokey—I hope this means we all walk out better than we walked in.

But the *main* reason I lift with the kids is to cut off one of their go-to excuses: *Why should I do this if you can't?* Our workouts are brutal by design. Football is often a game of sheer force, and strength plays a huge role. Our weight routine is designed to push the kids to their limit. Once they feel pressed up against that limit, many will look for any out they can find. By getting in there and getting my ass kicked too, I take one of their best excuses off the table.

Make no mistake. I *am* getting my ass kicked. Year after year, the players remain at the age of prime. I, however, get older. As this workout program—made for younger people with ambitious fitness goals—takes its toll on my aching bones, I increasingly wonder if I need to give up the ghost. I still believe there's value in me lifting with the kids…But at what cost to a middle-aged body?

Not too long ago, I came pretty close to calling it. Thanks to my basest instincts. I hate squats. In a football training setting, we squat with a weighted barbell on our shoulders. We do three sets of ten. The aim is progressive overload, meaning we want to lift enough weight that it hurts—and I mean *hurts*—to get to that tenth rep. I've hated weighted squats for as long as I can remember. I played football in college, until two broken vertebrae my sophomore year took me out of the game for good. I suppose the only immediate upside was that I was liberated from doing squats. From that moment on, I swore I'd never do them again.

Well, here I am nearly twenty-five years later, still doing squats. Surrounded by kids who've not yet experienced the wear and tear of time, who haven't yet learned that the human body is vulnerable and fallible.

In a recent workout, I was doing my third set of ten squat reps. I was silently resenting my promise to the boys to lift with them when I noticed…no one was watching me. My accountability partner had gone to get water. And everyone else, or so I thought, was focused on their own exercise. So what did I do? I stopped short. I racked my weights and let myself be done at nine. Because who cares, right?

Wrong.

"Coach," Rocco said. "How many was that?"

I hadn't noticed he had eyes on me. "Ten," I said.

"Lie!" Rocco declared.

Who does this kid think he is? I thought to myself. *Who the hell does he think he's talking to? I am their coach! I am a forty-three-year-old man. You think I need to be lifting in here with you? You think this matches my fitness goals? You think I'm doing this for me? Fine, kid, maybe this is the year I stop lifting with you. I don't need this.*

And then I smiled, wryly, to myself. Rocco was right. We'd all agreed to a culture of excellence, and I'd fallen short.

"The little matters a lot," I said to Rocco.

"That's right, Coach," he said, affirming our team's maxim.

I climbed my ass back under the bar and did one rep to get to ten and then two more. Because that's the standard and expectation in our weight room. You do the reps. And if you don't, you complete the reps you didn't do and tack on two more.

I had to laugh. I know the patterns of those who excel. And I know the pitfalls of those who don't. I know the reflexive reactions that hold people back from their potential, from trying hard and reaching ambitious goals. In the space of forty-five seconds, I exhibited all of them.

I lied. I blamed Rocco. I made excuses. And I threatened to quit. All because these behaviors felt better than viewing myself as weak, as capable of deceiving kids out of my own laziness, and as someone who can behave like a low achiever. I know loads about achievement, and I—still a human, still at the mercy of the lizard brain—get tripped up and fail to meet high expectations now and then.

―――

This is a book about performance—what it is and how to crack it. It's about the hidden inner work that must precede excellence. It's about how to get those persistent (but oh-so-human) pitfalls of low performance out of our way. It's about understanding the traps that pull us off track, learning which ones you're most vulnerable to, and identifying and practicing the behavioral patterns that will get you back on course. It's about shedding a mindset of low standards and wiring yourself a new one—one grounded in high expectations and the belief that you *can* do great things, that you *can* go the distance. One that prepares you to perform the way you want to in any endeavor—at the top of your game.

Ultimately, this is a book about everything I've learned about performance since I was a middle schooler playing competitive sports, a college athlete on the football field, a classroom teacher trying to light kids up, a CEO of my own small business, and an executive and leadership coach helping others forge their own paths to excellence. It's a collection of the knowledge I've gained from decades of inspecting, distilling, and unpacking performance in order to coach people to excel beyond their wildest dreams.

If you want to expose and purge your self-defeating thought patterns, those invisible habits of mind that are holding you back from achievements important to you, this book is for you. It will help you cultivate an inner ethos of excellence—that is, a guiding set of beliefs around how you relate to excellence in any domain that matters to you. Your health. Your work. Your parenting. Your relationships. Your hobby.

And here's the magic of this ethos: Once it's developed in one area, it tends to unlock a newfound sense of confidence and self-belief that will then naturally spill into other areas. For example: Nail your fitness routine, and you'll likely notice more sharpness and confidence at work. Apply the patterns of top performers in your parenting, and you will find yourself more capable of navigating sensitive conversations or situations in your work life, too. The specifics of your goals matter less to me than helping you build the mindset of top performers—the discipline, conviction, and clarity that drive achievement wherever you choose to apply it. The hidden work that top performers commit to daily, no matter what. The foundation that propels everyday effort into excellence.

This book rests on a core belief. Actually, let me call it what it is: a core *fact*. I've seen it play out too many times to call it anything less. Every single one of us is capable of excellence. Top performers aren't born—they're built. Sure, we've all got some raw talent, but talent alone has a low ceiling. It can only take you so far. Excellence is about discovering those talents and then *choosing* to live by the habits, standards, and mindset of top performers. It's about rejecting the habits that drag you down and replacing them with the ones that lift you up.

> Every single one of us is capable of excellence. Top performers aren't born—they're built.

I wouldn't be writing this if I didn't know this was true. And I wouldn't ask you to read it—to give of your valuable time—if I didn't believe *you* were capable of excellence. You absolutely are.

Because I believe that, my goal is to get you applying this work, not just absorbing it. This book is intentionally lean—designed with your time in mind. High performance doesn't happen in front of a book. It happens with customers, in classrooms, in boardrooms, on fields. It happens in how you show up, support others, and push through.

So, let's get to it.

CHAPTER 1

Choice: The Line Between Low and Top Performance

Are you smarter than an NFL quarterback?

Since leaving the classroom, I've been crisscrossing the country as a leadership and performance coach. I often speak with teachers about helping students excel. I speak with school and district leaders about driving performance across an entire school. More recently, I've been talking to business leaders about how performance culture directly impacts individual and collective results. No matter the audience, when I'm keynoting on performance, at some point I ask: "Are you smarter than an NFL quarterback?"

Don't worry—this book isn't about football, I swear. Stick with me a bit longer.

As a coach, teacher, and leader, there's nothing more gratifying than seeing your players, students, or colleagues go the distance. Little is more fun than catching up with them years later to hear how it's going.

A while back, I grabbed a drink with one of my former players. After graduating from the high school where I coach, he'd gone on to play tight end at Virginia Tech. After college, he was drafted by Bill Belichick and the New England Patriots.

As we caught up, our conversation drifted to the topic of the NFL Combine. Prior to the back injury sophomore year that ended my football career, I dreamed of participating in the Combine. Since I never got there, I've always been curious about it. The Combine is an annual event where top college players showcase their physical and mental abilities in front of NFL coaches, scouts, and executives. Until recently, it included timed drills like the 40-yard dash, vertical jump, and bench press, along with interviews and a test to help teams evaluate prospects before the draft.

For my former player, the Combine turned out to be pivotal. He was projected as a fifth-, sixth-, maybe even seventh-round draft pick. But he showed up, crushed it, and got drafted in the third round.

I asked him if he was nervous heading into the Combine. "Coach, I was so nervous about the Wonderlic test," he said.

I was stunned. *That's* what he was nervous about? Not only was he a great player, but he was also a really good student. Why would he be nervous about some football quiz? Well, it turns out, the Wonderlic has exactly zero football-related questions. The Wonderlic Contemporary Cognitive Ability Test—as it's formally called and named after its author, Eldon F. Wonderlic—is an intelligence test. It includes a mix of math, logic, verbal reasoning, and general knowledge questions. Think word problems, pattern recognition, basic algebra, vocabulary, and quick reading comprehension—all designed to test how fast and accurately someone can perform under pressure.

"It's fifty multiple choice questions. You have only twelve minutes to answer them, and you get one shot," he explained. A low score, as it turns out, can seriously hurt your draft chances.

The NFL is probably the test's most well-known client. Scores vary by position. Quarterbacks and offensive linemen—at least those who get drafted—tend to score higher, given the demands of their

CHOICE: THE LINE BETWEEN LOW AND TOP PERFORMANCE

roles. For reference, seven-time Super Bowl-winning quarterback Tom Brady scored a 33, which is considered a seriously impressive score. Quarterback Aaron Rodgers scored a 28, also strong. Only one player on record has scored a perfect 50: Pat McInally, a punter out of—you guessed it—Harvard. The average score across the Combine is 21. One of the most notorious Wonderlic stories is of a former North Carolina quarterback, Oscar Davenport. He was predicted to be a later-round draft pick—but the Wonderlic sank him. He scored a seven. For a quarterback—the position that requires the most clear thinking under intense scrutiny and pressure—that score proved career ending.

It's a tough test. Much tougher than I realized until my former player laid it out for me. Players have good reason to be nervous about the Wonderlic. The stakes are astronomically high.

But for a room of conference attendees, most of whom have likely never even stepped foot on a football field? The stakes couldn't be lower. And that's why I love to ask them if they're smarter than a quarterback. Because the answer couldn't matter less. But the exercise that follows, under the most minor of pressure, destabilizes most enough to activate classic low-performance behaviors. With this quick test, the little reveals a lot.

When I keynote, I'll share the story of my catch-up with my former player. Next up? You guessed it. I'll say to my audience, "That's right. Get out your phones. We're taking the Wonderlic!" I put a QR code on the screen for the audience to link to an online version of the test and instruct everyone to number a piece of paper 1 through 50.

By now, I've done this keynote enough times to see the same body language present in crowd after crowd. It's fascinating. There tend to be three types of reactions:

First, the competitors. These are the people who sit up straight—their shoulders are squared, they look focused. They're numbering their paper with haste and precision. You can almost hear them thinking, *Today's the day I beat Tom Brady at something.*

Next, the anxious achievers. They shift in their seats. Some glance nervously around, as if to gauge how seriously people are taking this or if others also seem nervous. Their brows might be furrowed. They might chew on their pens or mutter something under their breath. Their inner monologue goes something like, *OK, average score is 21. I just need to beat that. Please don't let me get shown up by a linebacker.*

And finally, the eye-rollers. They lean back, arms crossed, eyebrows raised. Maybe they scribble numbers half-heartedly or smirk at the QR code. To them, this is silly, they don't need this. Their vibe? *Whatever. As long as I don't score lower than that Oscar Davenport guy, I'm good.*

What I do next is highly choreographed, designed to create a frustrating, high-pressure environment for something that doesn't have any meaning or bearing on my audience's lives.

"We've all heard that if we write down a goal, we are more likely to achieve it. So on your paper, write down the score you want to achieve. Set a goal. Again, we're told setting a goal matters, so let's do it."

As I electronically release the test to them, I lay down the ground rules. By design, I have not yet told them to begin taking the test. "Number one, calculators are not allowed on the Wonderlic. Number two, and this is really important—there are no penalties for incorrect answers on the Wonderlic. Everyone pause what you're doing. Put eyes on me. There are no penalties for incorrect answers. Got it? No penalties for wrong answers. Lastly, we're on the honor system today. When you open the test, don't scroll to the first question—our twelve minutes haven't started yet." This causes people to look around and see what I'm seeing: Some people have already started taking the test. This happens every time. After all, this doesn't matter. What harm is a little jump-of-the-gun?

CHOICE: THE LINE BETWEEN LOW AND TOP PERFORMANCE

I'll continue. "Know that if you scroll to the bottom of the test, you'll see the answer key. I'm going to trust you all not to do that, OK?" Again, people look around, thinking what I'm also thinking—that plenty of people have already scrolled to the answer key.

I then repeat the rules. "No calculators. No penalties for wrong answers. No starting until I say so. No scrolling to the answer key."

One thing I never tell them yet—something I've already shared with you but that I don't mention in my keynote until after the audience takes the test: I haven't yet told them that, for the NFL, the Wonderlic is used to assess a player's ability to process information and act under pressure. I don't want to give the audience anything that can help them devise a strategy. I want them to go in as blind and as uncomfortable as possible. The only thing I do before we start the test is to tell them to relax and remind them that the stakes could not be lower. Then we're off to the races.

"All right. Ready? On your mark, get set, go!" The twelve-minute countdown begins.

Every two minutes, I update the audience. "Ten minutes remaining. That's ten minutes left." I do this as loudly and obnoxiously as I can. It jars the audience. Two minutes later. "Eight minutes, we've got eight minutes." Again, I'm startlingly loud. I'm grating on people. Tension in the room builds. "We're at six minutes. That's halfway through, everyone!" People shift in their seats, looking ever more anxious. "Four minutes! You're down to four minutes." At this point, I can tell people are really annoyed. Some are beginning to give up. "Two minutes remaining." The stress in the room is palpable. Then I get even more aggravating. "Sixty seconds! Just sixty seconds. That's one minute, people." With even more intensity in my voice, I say, "You've got just thirty more seconds. Thirty seconds left..." And finally, "Time! Pencils down. OK, everyone, on the honor system, grade your answers. Once you're done, write down your score next to the goal you set."

After a few minutes, I ask, "Did writing down a numeric goal have any material impact on how you performed on the test? Discuss with those around you." After a minute, I ask people to share their answers—which are always, "No, writing down a goal didn't matter a lick."

"But we're told this all the time. We're told all the time that writing down a goal will make us more likely to achieve it. But this didn't prove true today. Why?" I pause. "Because a goal without a plan is a wish. So my question for all of you—if writing down a goal had no impact, what would have? What would have helped you perform better on this test? Take sixty seconds, talk it over with your neighbors."

> Because a goal without a plan is a wish.

I let a little time pass. "Before I ask for shares, I want you to think about where your brain went when I asked what would have helped you do better. Chances are, you went to one of two places. You either focused on the circle of concern—those things that are concerning but that you have no control over. Or you focused on the circle of control—those things that are within your control to change or influence. In your conversation, I bet many people in this room said things like 'I wish I had more time.' Or 'I would have done better if there were fewer math questions.' More time and different questions would make it a completely different test, and these things don't concern us. The test is the test, and there's nothing we can change about it. Take a moment. Is what you shared with your neighbors circle of concern or circle of control issues? Recognize that if you're so focused on the circle of concern, you're ignoring the circle of control. Consider if this might be a reflex for you. This is important knowledge to file away. For now, let's put everything that's in the circle of concern on a shelf. What did you have control over that might have helped you perform better on the test?"

CHOICE: THE LINE BETWEEN LOW AND TOP PERFORMANCE

Once the audience is thinking in terms of what they themselves could have done differently, I ask for shares.

"I spent too much time on the math problems," someone will almost always say.

"Yes! Great answer," I'll say. "The twelve-minute timeframe of the Wonderlic adds pressure to the test. This is by design. One of the aims of the test is to assess how people make decisions when there's some kind of pressure on performance. Getting stuck on math questions instead of cutting your losses and moving forward is not the right strategy for the Wonderlic. As it turns out, the answers toward the end of the Wonderlic are designed to be quicker, so there's an advantage to getting through as many questions as fast as possible and then returning to the ones that stumped you. Making such a decision demonstrates quick thinking while against the clock." I'll then ask for more shares.

Inevitably, someone will say, "I have all these blank spaces on my answer sheet. I should have answered more questions."

"Yep. How many of you also have several blank spaces on your answer sheets?" Typically, about a third of the room raises their hands. "Why? What did I tell you three times? There are no penalties for wrong answers. What should have been the strategy?"

"When you said we had a minute left, we should have just randomly picked answers for questions we hadn't yet gotten to," someone will say.

"Bingo. You can pick up an extra five or so points just by guessing on the Wonderlic," I'll say, to a collective groan in the room. I will almost always hear someone say to a neighbor, "You should have told us that!" Which is perfect. That's exactly what I want. Finally, I explain to the audience why I just put them through the Wonderlic—especially in the obnoxious way that I did.

I love using games and challenges in my work, whether I'm keynoting about performance or coaching on the field or in a professional setting. They're a powerful way to surface the deeper patterns that affect how people show up under pressure. When a challenge feels real—even if the stakes are low—it tends to reveal two things: how a person approaches performance when it counts, and how they justify or cope with underperforming. Once I understand this about the people with whom I'm working, we can build a plan to avoid their personal performance pitfalls and instead go for excellence.

I've used the Wonderlic hundreds of times in my work, and the same four performance pitfalls emerge every time. People will take the test, and many don't perform the way they'd hoped. Whether it's kids or adults, most people respond in one or more of four ways:

They blame. When I keynote, I'll ask the participants who is most to blame for their low performance. Most everyone points to me. I didn't give them prep time, they'll say. I didn't explain the point of the test. I shouted out loud and annoying time warnings that broke their focus. All true, and I did this all on purpose. Why? Because distraction is part of life. So is being asked to perform without warning and under pressure. I want to see who can lock in and stay there, despite surprise and disruption. And I want to see who looks for someone to blame when they disappoint themselves.

They make excuses. This one is really common: People will say they didn't have enough time. I remind them that, on the Wonderlic, the time is fixed, it's in the circle of concern. It's a constraint under which we're all operating. The question is what you do inside that constraint. Another favorite excuse? This test came out of left field, people will say, and they weren't warmed up. They haven't had their coffee yet, as if the conditions need to be perfect for us to perform. Spoiler: they never are.

They deceive. With kids, deception is usually cheating—glancing at someone else's paper, sneaking over to the calculator app on their tablet despite the fact that it's forbidden on the Wonderlic. With adults, it's more subtle, but the goal is the same: deceive themselves so they may deceive others into a perception they're better or worse than they are. Adults will round up their score. They say they got a 27 when it was really a 21. (Or, *ahem*, they might say they completed all ten reps when they really did nine.) I also often hear people say they're "just not good at tests." This form of deception is to lower expectations, for themselves and in front of others. This way, low performance becomes expected and disappointment can be avoided. This kind of deception gets people off the hook categorically for things they believe they're not good at. But this precludes them from discovering a hidden strength, or that they've grown in an area they believed they never would, or an opportunity to improve in a way that can unlock new potential. What good does this do them?

They give up. This one's especially telling. Most kids take the test. Some finish, some don't—but they try. Adults? When I announce in a keynote that we're all going to take the Wonderlic, it's not uncommon for a few people to bow out before they even begin. They step out to take a call, or say they need the restroom—whatever the reason, these people decide they just don't need to play this dumb game. For those who stick around, there's still a sizable number who give up. Most people, kids and adults, need the full twelve minutes to complete the Wonderlic, but when I announce the first two-minute warning, people shift in their chairs. The ones who aren't performing as well as they'd hoped start to disengage. Their body language changes—shoulders slump, pacing slows, eyes wander. By the midway point, many of those same people put down their pencils. They're not out of time. They're just not hitting the score they imagined they would, so they tap out. *This doesn't actually matter, so forget it.*

Each of these responses reveals something deeper:

- When we blame, we outsource our agency.
- When we make excuses, we disempower ourselves.
- When we deceive ourselves or others, we sidestep self-honesty and miss a chance to improve.
- And when we give up, we lose the opportunity to grow. We don't just underperform—we opt out of performance altogether.

Every one of these behaviors says something about a person's self-belief, about the standards they've set for themselves. Each one points to a form of low expectation. And we all know the old adage: *Whether we think we can or can't—we're right.*

Outside the NFL Combine, the Wonderlic doesn't matter. It won't change anyone's life prospects. So why does something with such low stakes provoke such strong reactions and lead so many people straight into the trap of low performance? Why do we blame, make excuses, deceive, or give up—often without even realizing we're doing it—when low performance won't change outcomes?

Because underperformance can *feel* like a very real threat to our sense of self, even when it's not.

On some level, rationalizing our low performance is safer than confronting the truth. That drive to protect ourselves—and not just our physical selves but our self-perception, too—is as old as humankind.

> On some level, rationalizing our low performance is safer than confronting the truth.

To understand the roots of performance pitfalls, we must look back—way back—to the evolutionary wiring that shaped the human brain. Long before survival was a matter of earning enough money to afford shelter, clothing, food, and some leisure time with friends and family, survival depended on staying in good standing with the group. Early humans roamed in small, tightly bound tribes. Today, modern technologies and conveniences mean most people can figure out how to survive on their own. This would make for a joyless and difficult life, but it would be survivable nonetheless. This was not the case with prehistoric humans. Tens of thousands of years ago, it was unlikely that one could find and maintain shelter; hunt, kill, and prepare all food; raise children; defend oneself from predators; and constantly migrate, adjust, adapt, and stay alive amid changing weather all on one's own.

For prehistoric humans, survival required living and moving with the group. To be exiled from it wasn't just lonely; it was lethal. You simply couldn't survive without the protection and cooperation of the group. So every action, every signal, every perception from others seriously mattered.

Competence was not a matter of respect; it was a matter of maintaining your position in the group. If you were seen as capable, resourceful, steady under pressure, you had value. If you were perceived as weak, clumsy, unreliable, you became a liability. And if you became a liability, the group had a decision to make: carry your weight, or cut you loose. Life was about what was best for the pack. If you were deemed dead weight, you were likely soon, well, dead.

No wonder our nervous systems developed a reflexive sensitivity to any signal that might suggest we're falling short. When we underperform, even in a low-stakes setting like the Wonderlic in a conference, a primitive alarm bell goes off: *You're not measuring up! Your safety is under threat!* That sense of threat, that possibility of not being good enough gets processed as a risk that you could be cast off from the group, left to survive in the wild on your own. So to neutralize that risk, we react. We protect ourselves the only ways we know how:

- We blame. *It wasn't my fault.*
- We make excuses. *The conditions were unfair.*
- We deceive. *It didn't really happen the way you think it did.*
- We give up. *If I can't win, I won't try. The risks are too great.*

In prehistoric terms, these behaviors aren't weaknesses—they are logical defense mechanisms, designed to help preserve your standing in the group so you wouldn't get kicked out.

You can almost imagine a prehistoric human showing some weakness on the plains and applying any of these defense mechanisms. Maybe this person's role was to stand guard throughout the night while the others slept. Maybe this person dozed off, allowing a predator to enter the grounds and eat all the food that took several people and days to hunt and prepare. You can imagine this person desperately trying to negotiate away this catastrophic slip-up with any of the four performance pitfalls, pleading to be allowed to stay in the tribe.

Here, the pleading is completely rational. Convince the group you weren't to blame, and you survive. Fail to convince them? You get kicked out and very likely meet an early demise.

But in modern life? Are the four performance pitfalls rational? They are certainly *reflexive*, vestigial habits hard-wired into our primitive brain to keep us safe out on the plains.

But there's the problem: We're not on the plains anymore.

In most modern environments, our survival doesn't hinge on flawless performance or peer approval. No one's getting banished from the tribe for scoring a 19 on the Wonderlic (well, not those of us not trying out for the NFL, anyway). No matter the context of the Wonderlic, the stakes aren't life or death, yet our brain treats them that way. The reflexes that once helped us survive now, in the modern world, get in our way. They convince us to protect our pride instead of pursue our potential. They push us to avoid discomfort instead of growing through it. They tell us to choose the warmth of the known and familiar over calculated risks—even the kinds that excellence requires.

When we cave to those old instincts, we miss out. Not just on a better score or a better outcome, but on the chance to build something better in ourselves. We miss the opportunity to get honest, take ownership, learn from the misses, and keep going.

Blame might feel safe. Excuses might feel justified. Deception might even feel smart. Giving up can sure feel easier. But every time we—modern humans living not on the plains but in comfortable and generally safe lives—respond in these ways, we're choosing comfort over growth, stagnation over excellence.

First, let's be gracious with ourselves. The pitfalls of performance are normal. They are deeply human. Everyone employs them at some point or another. We might even reflexively and, if only for split seconds, default to them daily. These are habits designed to keep us alive, so let's not beat ourselves up for being human and having a drive to survive.

But let's also see those pitfalls for what they are: obsolete and, therefore, a red herring. They are neither real nor necessary in our modern lives. When they become our default mode, we're letting a primordial habit, not a conscious decision, run the hard drive. We're staying stuck in the circle of concern. We're blaming our primitive brain, as if we're at its mercy. But the primitive brain is gonna primitive brain no matter what. So we must make a conscious choice not to live from our ancient wiring.

Let's take this excuse of the primitive brain off the table. As I ask my audience to do with their frustration that the Wonderlic's time is fixed at twelve minutes, let's shelve the primitive brain. Better yet, let's develop a sense of humor about it. When it compels us to do something like, oh…you know…lie to a high school student over how many reps you did and then blame said kid for it, let's laugh. Because it *is* absurd. Then let's immediately move forward.

Top performance is about consciously choosing to get off the ancient plains, so to speak, and into our present reality. When you catch yourself defaulting to a low-performance pitfall, smile. And then pause to appraise the moment: Are you actually under threat? Could this thing in front of you that feels hard and demands more from you *kill* you? Ninety-nine percent of the time, the answer is no—thank goodness! You are safe. So acknowledge that the threat isn't real.

So what *is* real? The opportunity before you—the opportunity to perform better, do better, be better is there, calling you, just waiting for you to seize it.

Once we recognize and avoid the trap, we can choose a better path. A path rooted not in survival but in performance. Not in the instinct to protect but in the willingness to pursue.

Let's talk about what that path looks like.

Here's the great thing about the four performance pitfalls: Their opposites are obvious. Each is one side of a coin whose inverse holds the key:

- The opposite of blame is *ownership*.
- The opposite of making excuses is identifying *solutions*.
- The opposite of self-deception or delusion is *self-confrontation*.
- The opposite of giving up is *grit*.

If each performance pitfall is prehistoric reflex, then each pattern of top performance is merely a conscious choice.

TOP-PERFORMANCE PATTERNS			
Ownership	Solutions	Self-Confrontation	Grit
Blame	Excuses	Self-Deception	Giving Up
LOW-PERFORMANCE PITFALLS			

I use the terms *pitfalls* and *patterns* deliberately. Pitfalls are the default thoughts and behaviors we fall into when we're not paying attention—automatic responses shaped by our prehistoric wiring. They're built-in, ever-present, and easy to trigger. Like landmines, they don't require intention, just inattention. But once we become aware of

CHOICE: THE LINE BETWEEN LOW AND TOP PERFORMANCE

them, we can start stepping around them. Awareness is step one. Step two is substitution—replacing those reflexive behaviors with conscious ones. That's where patterns come in.

Patterns are practiced. They're choices we make, over and over again, until they become habits. And while we can never fully override our ancient wiring—nor should we—we *can* train our brain to reserve those snap, self-protective reactions for moments of real danger. The rest of the time, we need to choose differently. We need to move with intention. We need to rely on the learned, repeatable behaviors that drive growth, resilience, and sustained excellence. That's what top performers do—not once, not twice, but consistently, day in, day out.

No, your survival doesn't depend on choosing the patterns of top performance. But the stakes are still extremely high.

Let's look at it this way: When it comes to the Wonderlic, those low-performance pitfalls don't actually matter. Who cares how you did on a test you'll forget ten minutes later?

But when it comes to what those pitfalls reveal about how you show up for the things that *do* matter? The important relationships, the chances you take (or don't), the effort you put into building a meaningful life? Then the stakes couldn't be higher.

To live a life defined by the pitfalls of low performance—blame, excuses, self-deception, giving up—might not kill you. But it can still be tragic.

―――

OK, I admit—that's a little dramatic. But so is reaching the end of your life and realizing you didn't live it the way you could have. Let the drama fuel you. Let the fear of existential regret give you the push you need to make sure you choose *today* to live the life you want to see when you look back on it.

I don't mean chasing material success. I mean taking calculated risks. Testing your mettle. Going outside your comfort zone and growing as a result. When you look back one day, it won't be the car you drove or the house you bought that mattered. These things may come as a result of your performance. But in study after study—whether in the final moments of life or in the reflections of those who came near death—the regrets are crystal clear:

- You'll wish you took ownership instead of blaming others.
- You'll wish you searched for solutions instead of hiding behind excuses.
- You'll wish you had gotten honest with yourself, instead of wasting away in comforting untruths.
- And you'll wish you had just *tried*, for the love of God—even if you still failed.

This book is your blueprint to a life well lived. It's a handbook for how to remove yourself from the circle of concern and plant yourself firmly in the circle of control—the *only* place from which you are empowered. It's a simple plan to pattern your daily choices after those who achieve at the top of their game. It's a guide to prevent those end-of-life regrets and instead look back on a life that was rich in personal evolution, expansion, growth, meaning, and courage.

I promise you, it's easier than you think.

CHAPTER 2

Ownership: The Antidote to Blame

TOP-PERFORMANCE PATTERNS

Ownership   Solutions   Self-Confrontation   Grit

If you've never watched *Shark Tank*, you're missing the business world's version of a high-stakes playoff game—strategy, stakes, and million-dollar decisions in real time.

Shark Tank premiered in 2009 and has been a sensation ever since. Entrepreneurs-turned-contestants in search of funding walk into "the tank" to pitch their product to five investors known as the Sharks. Their goal is to convince at least one Shark to invest in their company. It's part strategy, part storytelling, part survival—and pure performance.

Entrepreneurs get just a few minutes to explain what they've built, prove their market, sell their numbers, and make a compelling ask—usually while being grilled by wildly successful, brutally honest investors. The Sharks will challenge forecasts, scrutinize strategies, and poke holes in assumptions. Sometimes the questions get personal, like if a founder can juggle startup life with a full-time job. The pressure is intense. The pace is fast. And the stakes are high.

When a pitch shows promise, a Shark might offer to invest in exchange for equity. Sometimes Sharks will get into a bidding war. Other times, no one bites, and the entrepreneur is sent home empty handed. No matter the outcome, that moment in the tank is not the end of the story. In fact, it's where the real test begins.

Entrepreneurs who land an investment still must prove they are worthy of it. They have to turn that money into traction, revenue, and sustainable growth—no small task. But the entrepreneurs I've always been most interested in are the ones the Sharks reject, the ones who walk out with nothing but a bruised ego. Because if they still believe in their idea, they must do everything the funded entrepreneurs do—but without the cash, and after getting told on national television that their pitch wasn't good enough. That's a defining moment. How they respond tells us everything.

One of the most well-known underdog stories to come out of *Shark Tank* is that of Jamie Siminoff, the founder of Ring. Back in 2013, he pitched a smart video doorbell—then called DoorBot—to the Sharks. While he did get one offer, Jamie was hesitant about the terms. He and the Shark couldn't find common ground, so the Shark pulled his offer, and Jamie walked away without a deal. And what of the other Sharks? They weren't exactly bullish. Some didn't see the market or value. One questioned the pricing and sustainability of the technology. By and large, they just didn't buy the pitch.

But Siminoff didn't fold his hand and give up. He may have lost the round, but he didn't believe he'd lost the game. He took the Sharks' feedback seriously. He rebranded, refined the product, and kept building. Fast forward to 2018, and Amazon acquired Ring for over an eye-popping one *billion* dollars. (Regrets? Yes, some Sharks have a few!)

So how does something like that happen? What allows someone not just to recover from rejection—and a very public one at that—but

OWNERSHIP: THE ANTIDOTE TO BLAME

also grow even more convicted in his or her vision and go on to win? I'd wondered about this for years—until, as luck would have it, I got to ask a Shark myself.

Barbara Corcoran is one of the original Sharks—the real estate powerhouse who turned a one-thousand-dollar loan into a multi-million-dollar empire. She doesn't mince words. She has a sixth sense for weakness, and if you get defensive or dodge responsibility, she'll call it out instantly. But she's also quick to reward confidence, clarity, and ownership. She can spot BS in five seconds flat and still root for your success if you're self-aware and want to improve.

A few years ago, Corcoran and I were speaking at the same conference. As we sat in the green room together, we chatted about life and work. All the while, in the back of my mind I was thinking about her time on *Shark Tank*. In my head I thought, "Don't ask about *Shark Tank*. Don't be that guy. She's always asked about *Shark Tank*. Resist, Kieschnick!" Moments later, I found myself doing exactly what I swore I wouldn't…I asked her about *Shark Tank*.

"I'm super interested in the people who *don't* get a deal on *Shark Tank*," I said. "When you look at all the entrepreneurs who've left without a deal, what's the difference between those who go on to create successful businesses and those we never hear from again?"

She didn't hesitate: "The people who go on to create successful businesses after not getting a deal—they're the people who walk out of the room without blaming the Sharks. They look at themselves. They take the feedback. They think, 'My pitch wasn't clear enough.' Or 'I didn't communicate my vision or my customers well enough.' They don't blame the Sharks. Instead, they look internally for why they didn't get the external result."

Barbara's insight didn't just resonate, it rewired something in me. The people who go on to succeed don't leave the tank pointing fingers, they leave asking questions. They reflect. They ask what *they* could've done better. In doing so, they set themselves up for growth. This shift—from blaming others to self-reflection—is packed with potential. Yet it can be rare. Many avoid the shift and give up by default.

The Psychology Behind Blame

If we really pause to think about it, we know that blaming others for our lackluster performance won't make us better. So why do we indulge a behavior that's sure to keep us stuck? Why is our first instinct so often to deflect, to blame?

It comes down to that prehistoric drive to survive. Blaming others feels like the safer bet, at least at first. If we mess up and can convince the tribe it wasn't our fault, then we stand a better shot of remaining safely in the group. But if we take ownership, we are admitting a mistake, perhaps even a fault. We risk being banished and left to survive on our own.

At the core of human instinct is a fundamental fear of death. Tens of thousands of years ago, our central motivation was to avoid threats to our lives—threats that were immediate, physical, and constant. But today, most of us no longer face the same daily dangers our prehistoric ancestors did. Our nervous systems, however, haven't fully caught up.

Instead of physical predators, we now fear social and professional exclusion. Rather than fight to survive in the wild, we fight to maintain belonging in the groups that shape our personal and professional lives. These groups may not determine our physical survival, but they are vital to our psychological survival—our sense of identity, purpose, and worth.

Psychologists Jeff Greenberg, Tom Pyszczynski, and Sheldon Solomon call this *terror management theory*.[1] Their research shows that because humans are uniquely aware of our mortality, we live under a constant, if subconscious, existential anxiety. In ancient times, this anxiety was buffered by physical preparedness—the ability to hunt, fight, protect. Today, that buffer is self-esteem.

OWNERSHIP: THE ANTIDOTE TO BLAME

In modern life, survival isn't just about physical strength; it's also about psychological strength. It's about feeling like we matter. Self-esteem serves as our internal signal that we have value in the groups we care about. It affirms our belief that we are contributing members of a meaningful whole. The higher our self-esteem, the more confident we are that we won't be rejected or cast out.

When failure enters the picture—especially when others witness that failure—it threatens our buffer. Our self-esteem takes a hit, and with it goes our sense of psychological safety. Suddenly, we're not just dealing with a mistake; we're dealing with what that mistake might mean about us and our futures. We fear that others will question our value or capability. Worse, we fear they might be right.

This is where blame steps in. From the perspective of terror management theory, blame can be understood as a reflexive effort to protect the self from the psychological discomfort of diminished self-esteem. If we can attribute the failure to someone or something outside of ourselves—a teammate, a boss, a bad system—we can preserve our self-worth and evade the deeper, often painful confrontation with our own inadequacy.

Greenberg, Pyszczynski, and Solomon's work helps us see this not as weakness but as a deeply human response to a primal fear. Our impulse to defend ourselves, even irrationally, is an evolutionary strategy to maintain standing within the group and avoid being ostracized. From this angle, blame isn't about truth; it's about control. When outcomes feel out of our control, we can latch onto blame to regain a sense of stability and agency, even if that agency is built on dishonesty and deflection.

The cost of this sense of protection is steep. When we default to blame, we bypass the process of learning. In a series of studies from Carol Tavris and Elliot Aronson, authors of *Mistakes Were Made (But Not by Me)*, participants who blamed others after making a mistake were significantly less likely to digest constructive feedback or change their understanding.[2] Here, blame defeats us twice—we give away our agency *and* give up our ability to learn. We miss the opportunity to examine our role in what happened, gain insight, and then adapt and improve. When we hold onto the version of ourselves that never fails, it keeps us from becoming someone who learns how to succeed.

We can imagine how this might have played out on the ancient plains. Let's return to the prehistoric man from chapter 1—the one assigned to stand guard while the rest of the group slept. He falls asleep. A bear enters the camp and is free to eat the meat the tribe had spent days hunting, preparing, and storing. When morning comes and the group discovers the loss, this man has a choice. He can deflect—blame the cold, the darkness, the fatigue, the bear itself. Or he can take ownership. Yes, admitting fault carries risk. But it also opens the door to improving the group's system. It invites the group to ask better questions: Should there have been a second guard? Was the fire too low? Was the food stored too low to the ground? In taking responsibility, not only does the man learn, but he also enables the entire group to learn. His ownership becomes an act of leadership. And, over time, that earns trust in a way blame never will.

All told, blame comes with a deep and self-defeating irony: We use it to protect ourselves, yet over time it can make us feel less secure. It can even make our peers less secure. When blame becomes habitual, it blocks us from learning and adapting. We stagnate. And as the gap between our performance and our potential widens, we do, in fact, risk becoming less valuable to the teams, communities, and networks on which we depend. As a result, they also stand to lose when we lose value. The very behavior meant to preserve our sense of self-worth and psychological safety can end up undermining both.

> When blame becomes habitual, it blocks us from learning and adapting.

OWNERSHIP: THE ANTIDOTE TO BLAME

It can get worse from there. Research from social psychologist Roy Baumeister and colleagues has shown that routinely avoiding responsibility can diminish intrinsic motivation.[3] When we give into the pitfall of blame repeatedly, we teach ourselves that our actions don't matter and that forces beyond our control dictate our outcomes. This mindset breeds passivity, and passivity kills potential. Rather than trying again with greater clarity or effort, we retreat—often repeating the same mistakes without attempting to understand them, in a doom loop of failure that grows ever harder to extract ourselves from.

Mike Tomlin understands this intimately. He goes out of his way not to come within a football field's length of the failure doom loop. In 2007, at just thirty-four, Tomlin was named head coach of the Pittsburgh Steelers, where he remains at the helm as of this book's publication. In his second season as coach, he led the team to a Super Bowl victory, making him the youngest coach in NFL history to win the ring. He's never, not once, had a losing season—a nearly unmatched streak in the NFL. No surprise, he's one of the most respected leaders in the league, admired for his no-nonsense approach and extreme accountability.

One of the most potent drivers of Tomlin's performance ethos is his rigorous refusal to blame, no matter how uncomfortable it feels. On an episode of *The Pivot* podcast, he explains that those who love us often help us deflect responsibility in an attempt to shield us from pain.[4] After a loss, Tomlin shares, his mom will often say something like "The refs did us wrong." But to Tomlin, this "stings his ears." Because even well-intentioned blame is an entry point into the failure doom loop, where top performance slips further out of reach. As a leader, Tomlin knows he must model the behavior he expects from his players. So every day, he resists the pitfall of blame and lives the pattern of ownership so consistently that discomfort has become his default setting.

Blame is like a dopamine hit—a quick rush of self-protection that offers only temporary relief. And for what? A fleeting sense of security that ultimately separates us from our agency. Blame robs us of the feedback we need to grow. It keeps our focus stuck on what we can't control instead of empowering us to act on what we can. And if you spend your life avoiding the temporary discomfort of ownership, you won't build the lasting muscle of accountability. You won't get better. You'll just get better at blaming.

> Blame is like a dopamine hit—a quick rush of self-protection that offers only temporary relief. And for what? A fleeting sense of security that ultimately separates us from our agency.

Ownership: A Pattern of Top Performers

Serena Williams was preparing for a semifinal match at the September 2015 US Open. She was set to face off against Roberta Vinci, a low-ranked player who had never beaten Williams and wasn't expected to make it past the early rounds. Williams was a 300-to-1 favorite to win. These weren't just odds in Williams's favor; they screamed foregone conclusion.

So far that year, Williams had already won the Australian Open, French Open, and Wimbledon. This match should have been a formality on Williams's path to making history—a calendar Grand Slam: taking all four single Grand Slam titles in one calendar year, the kind of achievement that propels one to legend status, and something that only three female tennis players have achieved to this day.

But Williams lost.

It was one of the biggest upsets in tennis history. A loss so shocking that the media—and fans—seemed gripped with a collective cognitive dissonance. The press immediately searched for an explanation. Was it the pressure? The court? Williams's recent elbow injury? Surely there had to be something that could explain how the most dominant player in the game fell to a player she categorically outmatched.

When the media prodded and pressed and pressured Williams to make sense of a loss that made no sense, Williams didn't take the bait. When asked if her recent injury contributed to the loss, she said no. When given the chance to put down her opponent by saying she herself played poorly, she refused. "No," she said. "I don't think I played that bad. She [Vinci] played out of her mind. I made more unforced errors than I normally would make, but I think my opponent played really well."[5]

No deflection. No blame. No reaching for a narrative to protect her ego. Just clarity, candor, and respect—not just for herself but also for her opponent. And all this amid crushing heartbreak.

Now that's ownership.

———

As it turns out, even Serena Williams is a mere mortal. Her losses are rare, but they happen. Even in the face of failure, her patterns of top performance remain firmly intact. She never gives into the pitfalls. It would have been so easy for Williams to blame her injury, and every person watching would've nodded along, relieved to hear an explanation for an inconceivable loss. But she didn't. This is because, like every top performer, Williams knows—when you own your performance, you also own what comes next.

Ownership is the ability to stand in the reality of your outcomes— good *and* bad—and claim your role in them with honesty and objectivity. It means resisting the pull of defensiveness and blame and instead getting curious and asking, *What was within my control? What could I have done better or differently? Where do I need to improve?*

From a psychological perspective, ownership rests on the foundational belief that our actions are always relevant. They always matter. You've heard me call this the circle of control—those factors we can influence and that impact outcomes—as opposed to the circle of concern. Psychologist Julian Rotter called it *locus of control*. This idea refers to whether we see outcomes as primarily the result of our own behavior (internal locus) or the result of forces outside our control (external locus).[6]

People with an internal locus of control tend to take more initiative, persevere longer, and manage setbacks productively. Why? Because when you believe you have an innate capacity to impact the direction of your life, you're more likely to act like it. Over the course of a life, this pays off. Decades of research have shown that people with a strong internal locus of control perform better academically, earn more over their lifetimes, recover faster from failures and distress, and even live longer.

By contrast, those with an external locus believe they are at the mercy of everything beyond them, with no ability to direct the outcomes of their lives. Instead, their lives are a matter of luck (good or bad), timing, or others' actions. They are more likely to disengage, give up, or be passive in the face of difficulty. And who can blame them? Why try if trying will get you nowhere?

Top performers won't go near an external locus. They see it for what it is: a performance *and* future killer. To blame is to stagnate, and nothing is more excruciating to top performers than stagnation. When things go wrong, they want both to understand why and mine a disappointment for insights that can help them perform better in the future. So they look *inward*.

But they don't stop there: When things go right, they look *around*—acknowledging teammates, timing, even luck. This is the opposite of what researchers call the *self-serving bias*, which is the tendency to take credit for success and blame others for failure. Here again, top performers set themselves apart. They turn self-serving bias on its head. This is sometimes called *extreme ownership*, where top performers know it's not enough to own their losses; they know they must also own their wins. They understand that growth requires taking full responsibility for their failures, but stratospheric growth demands that they consider the external factors that contributed to their successes. Meaning, they own only the *internal* locus aspects of their win and give credit to all the *external* locus aspects where it's due—externally. In doing so, they can plan for a future where those external factors may no longer be present to give them a boost and prepare to excel without them. Even wins offer an opportunity to do better next time.

You can bet Serena Williams lives the ethos of extreme ownership. After beating American Kristie Ahn in the 2020 French Open, she expressed disappointment in her *victory*. The first set of the match progressed to a tie-break. Williams was able to tip the scales in her favor, but she was frustrated that she allowed a tie to happen at all. In an interview after the match, she said she needed to work on the mental part of her game.

This is not at all to say we shouldn't celebrate our wins—we absolutely should. Extreme ownership is simply a reminder not to rest on your laurels. If you believe your wins are personal and your losses are circumstantial, you never truly improve. Ownership corrects for that bias. It teaches us to examine both our wins and our losses with a critical eye—not to inflate or diminish our role but to understand it.

While growth cannot happen without ownership, the irony, of course, is that ownership can feel terrifying—literally, at that instinctive, evolutionary level of fearing for our safety. But this is where we, if we want to pursue the patterns of top performers, must consciously dispense with our ancient wiring and choose a new pattern. Yes, to take ownership is to expose your fallibility, gaps, and imperfections. But in practice and effect, ownership is a form

> In the end, ownership is an essential ingredient of what separates performers who grow from those who stall.

of strength. Not to mention, it puts you in an elite class with the Serena Williamses and Mike Tomlins of the world. It's from this mindset of elite performers that we can improve.

In the end, ownership is an essential ingredient of what separates performers who grow from those who stall. Not raw talent. Not lucky breaks. Not favorable circumstances. But a willingness to take responsibility for what's theirs—the good, the bad, the ugly—and get better because of it.

———

When Jamie Siminoff walked out of the Shark Tank studio in 2013, he went straight back to his garage, where he ran his small DoorBot operation, and got back to work—devastated and defeated. He was crestfallen that he left without a deal. His business was teetering on the brink, and he needed cash. He resisted the urge to blame the Sharks, despite how easy it would have been. Instead, he maintained ownership of his fate and kept his nose to the grindstone. But don't be fooled by Ring's eventual one-billion-dollar sale to Amazon—his path to this astronomical achievement was by no means easy.

In 2018, when Amazon announced its purchase, Siminoff gave an interview to *Inc.* magazine. He said:

> The years 2015 to 2017 might have been the toughest. If I'd stopped, I would have lost my house. I had a 3-year-old and the only thing I could do was keep trying. There were nights when I woke up at 3 a.m. in tears. Bawling. How were we going to make it to tomorrow? Luckily, no matter how mentally hard that was, I had one choice, which was "Pick yourself up, Jamie, and get back out there." Because stopping would have resulted in the end.

OWNERSHIP: THE ANTIDOTE TO BLAME

People used to ask me, "What would you do differently?" I'd say, "Raising $100 million right off the bat would have been much better." They would kind of look at me like, "Why didn't you?" Well, I didn't because nobody would give me a friggin' $100 million. Someone else said to me, "I heard a fund pulled out of one of your rounds." A fund? Try 250 funds! I wish it had been one fund. Everybody pulled out of my rounds.[7]

Jamie took hit after hit, blow after blow, and still got up and pushed on. He did not blame others for his string of disappointments. He refused to outsource his agency and hold anyone else accountable for his future but him. To say it paid off is an understatement.

Blame is reactive. Ownership is proactive.

Blame says, "This happened to me." Ownership says, "This happened because of me—or in spite of me—and I still have a role to play in what happens next." Blame avoids. Ownership accepts.

Blame is easy in the moment but toxic over time. Ownership is hard in the moment but transformational over time.

And the choice is always yours.

> Blame is easy in the moment but toxic over time. Ownership is hard in the moment but transformational over time.

CHAPTER 3

Solutions: Escaping the Excuse Trap

TOP-PERFORMANCE PATTERNS

Ownership   **Solutions**   Self-Confrontation   Grit

B*ack in 2011, I was coaching educators and administrators on instructional best practices and delivering keynotes on blended learning.* In simplest terms, blended learning refers to using technology to enhance instruction and student learning outcomes, not just for the sake of using it. At the time, and still too often, much of the tech in schools was performative—devices were purchased for optics, not impact, leading to millions of dollars spent with almost nothing to show for it.

Nonetheless, as students move into middle and high school, tech fluency is a must. Denying students access to the tools used in nearly every modern career is denying them opportunity.

Joe Casarez understood this. When we met in 2011, he'd just been named assistant superintendent of Coalinga-Huron Unified School District in California's Central Valley—one of the poorest districts in the state. With a per capita income around $22,000, nearly 30% of families live in poverty, many of them migrant farmworkers whose children experience constant disruption in their schooling.[1]

THE HIDDEN WORK

When Joe arrived, the district had recently purchased $1 million worth of MacBooks and iPads—a great development, as most of his students had never used a laptop and were desperate to learn how. But the teachers never received any training on how to integrate the devices into instruction, so the laptops remained in storage collecting dust. Joe was determined to change this. After hearing me keynote, he invited me in to coach his educators.

For several months, I spent time in classrooms alongside teachers who were eager to learn—and even more eager to help their students. Together, we made plans to build students' tech fluency and—the main goal of blended learning—boost their performance and skill development. We did this through intentional tech use in the classroom and meaningful homework for the kids to complete on their laptops after school.

There was just one problem: No one had Wi-Fi at home. In fact, there was barely any Wi-Fi in the entire town. Outside of the schools, the only public internet access in Coalinga-Huron was at the local McDonald's. Not even the library had connectivity.

Joe and his team started brainstorming solutions. Meanwhile, some students came up with their own.

Each day, I noticed the same pack of kids walking to McDonald's after school—but never going in. Instead, they'd sit outside, backs against the building. When I asked Joe what these kids were doing, he teared up. They were doing their homework, he explained. The McDonald's manager had told them they couldn't go inside unless they bought something. Some of these kids lived in homes without indoor plumbing; daily McDonald's purchases were out of the question. So the students and the manager struck a deal: The kids would stay outside and not cause trouble, and they could keep using the Wi-Fi.

That image—kids hunched over homework on bare concrete—burned itself into my memory and never left. These students weren't waiting for the system to solve the problem. They were solving it themselves.

Now, not all the students did this. Many came to school with unfinished homework along with the perfectly valid reason that they had no internet at home. But in the face of the same constraint, some kids forged a different path.

Joe did, too. He and his team eventually landed on a solution that was both simple and brilliant: They outfitted every school bus with Wi-Fi. Students could work during their commutes. Then, when the buses weren't in use, the drivers parked them strategically around town, turning the district's own fleet into a rolling network of hotspots.

Nearly fifteen years later, I still think about those kids outside McDonald's. They had an intuitive grasp on one of the most important patterns of top performance: They did not make excuses. Instead, they looked for solutions.

Excuses: The Quiet Exit from the Arena

In 1910, just off his second and final term, President Theodore Roosevelt spent a year traveling the world speaking about character, responsibility, and the moral obligation to strive for something bigger than oneself. In Paris, he delivered the most famous address of the tour, "Citizenship in a Republic," to a packed hall at the Sorbonne, one of France's oldest and most prestigious universities.

Buried in the middle of that speech was a passage that would outlive all the others. Over a century later, it's still recited in locker rooms, boardrooms, graduation speeches. You've probably heard it before. It goes like this (emphasis mine):

> It is not the critic who counts; not the man who points out how the strong man stumbles, or where the doer of deeds could have done them better. **The credit belongs to the man who is**

actually in the arena, whose face is marred by dust and sweat and blood; who strives valiantly; who errs, who comes short again and again, because there is no effort without error and shortcoming; but who does actually strive to do the deeds; who knows great enthusiasms, the great devotions; who spends himself in a worthy cause; who at the best knows in the end the triumph of high achievement, and who at the worst, if he fails, at least fails while daring greatly.[2]

If you've ever heard reference to "the man in the arena," this speech is its origin. This excerpt is one of those rare passages that transcends space and time. It's the kind of rhetoric that can cut straight to the heart and deliver the exact point you need to hear at that exact moment. It feels both completely personal and universally relevant. No matter the specific motivation an individual might take from it, ultimately this speech is about getting in the game—whatever the game is to you.

Brené Brown read the passage as a call to vulnerability—not as weakness but as courage: the choice to enter the arena of life with an open heart and nothing to hide. She was so moved by the idea that she built a whole framework around the passage's final words and recorded it in *Daring Greatly*, her book on the power of vulnerability in how we live, love, parent, and lead.[3]

Roosevelt's words don't just highlight vulnerability—they also draw a line in the sand. Between the brave and the bystanders. The ones who risk and the ones who ridicule. That line runs through every part of life: work, relationships, creativity, leadership, ambition. On one side: the critics, the excuse-makers, the disengaged. On the other: the ones willing to step forward, get messy, and fail, perhaps even publicly, for the chance to grow, for a shot at achieving something great.

The arena is not for the faint of heart. It's for people willing to sacrifice their pride, their perfectionism, and their self-image in service of something bigger. It's for people who understand that failure is never the enemy—comfort is. It's for those who know nothing worthwhile can be achieved while clinging to the myth of safety.

Yes, there's timeless wisdom, even poetry, in Roosevelt's words. But underneath all of it, what I hear is this: *Stop making excuses and get in the damn arena.*

———

Here's the real problem with excuses: They can be oh so subtle. If blame is a pointed finger, excuses are a shrug. *Blame demands attention. Excuses erode intention. Blame breaks trust. Excuses break momentum.*

Blame almost always comes with indignation. Blame can feel loud, accusatory. But excuses are small, even gentle. Blame is "The refs screwed us again!" Whereas an excuse is "We would have won if we weren't on the road." Or "I just didn't have enough practice time." Excuses show up not as confrontation but as quiet withdrawals—from effort, from risk, from possibility.

But don't be deceived by the docile facade of excuses. Like their louder, more hot-headed counterpart, blame, excuses are also a performance killer. Because every time you reach for one, you step further away from the arena where the action happens. Just one excuse is enough to take you out of the game. But a heaping pile of them puts you in the next town over from the arena.

Excuses aren't about casting fault onto someone or something else. They're about giving yourself a soft landing—a way to cut the tension of falling short. They let you exit early while telling yourself you're still capable. They don't lash out. They let you off the hook, leaving you feeling a kind of relief. And that's what makes them so insidious.

The Psychology Behind Excuses

Excuses generally serve a very specific purpose: to rid ourselves of the distress of cognitive dissonance. Cognitive dissonance, a concept introduced by social psychologist Leon Festinger in 1957, refers to the internal discomfort we feel when our behavior contradicts our beliefs about ourselves.[4] If I see myself as a confident communicator but I avoid speaking up in meetings or deflect questions when they come my way, that internal inconsistency creates discomfort. Or if I believe I'm a present, supportive parent, but I find myself constantly distracted on my phone during family time, that contradiction creates tension.

Enter excuses to resolve that tension: "I am a confident communicator, but I just don't want to dominate meetings. I don't want to make my coworkers uncomfortable." Or "I'm sitting right here on the playground with my kids; so what if I'm scrolling on my phone? How many parents take their kids to the park at all? Don't I deserve a mindless break, too? Zoning out now and then actually helps me be a more present parent."

The brain craves cohesion between who we think we are and how we behave. Knowing what we know now about how our ancient wiring works in the modern world, we understand how cognitive dissonance can trigger the existential alarm: When that cohesion breaks, we rush to stitch it back together to protect our self-perception and maintain a sense of psychological safety and security in our groups. One of the fastest ways to do this is to make an excuse. These explanations might provide relief by tricking us into thinking we've closed the gap between action and identity. But the relief is only temporary. Because an excuse does nothing to help us change the thing that created the cognitive dissonance in the first place.

An excuse is cheap. It's easy and delivered in mere seconds. But the costs are incredibly high. Instead of confronting the gap between our standards and our choices, we paper over it. We separate ourselves

SOLUTIONS: ESCAPING THE EXCUSE TRAP

from the work of finding a solution that would align our behaviors and beliefs. The longer we do this, the more the cognitive tension fades—not because we've resolved it, but because we've numbed ourselves to the discomfort and therefore robbed ourselves of the motivation to change. Excuses are down payments on staying stuck exactly where we are.

> Excuses are down payments on staying stuck exactly where we are.

Humans are so motivated to avoid the psychological destabilization of cognitive dissonance that we sometimes plan excuses in advance of something that might harm our self-image. In a now-classic 1978 study, psychologists Steven Berglas and Edward Jones set out to understand why people sometimes sabotage their own chances of success.[5] To test this, the researchers gave college students a logic test and then told some of them—regardless of how they performed—that they'd done exceptionally well.

This group of students who were told they over-performed were then told they'd take a second test. The researchers offered them a choice between two drugs. Berglas and Jones led participants to believe one drug would enhance performance and one would impair it. The drugs were fake, and neither they nor the second test was administered. The point was to log which drug the participants said they wanted and why. Those unsure of whether their exceptional performance was due to their own ability or just luck were more likely to choose the performance-impairing drug. Not because they wanted to do poorly but because it gave them an out. If they failed the next test, it wouldn't mean they were not smart—it would just mean the drug got in the way. Put another way, these participants had an external locus of control, where they felt disempowered and without agency over their performance. A performance-impairing drug would validate their external locus of control and excuse poor performance.

This phenomenon, which Berglas and Jones dubbed as *self-handicapping*, revealed something profound about human behavior: We will sometimes trade honest performance for psychological protection. We'd rather underperform for a pre-canned reason than give our best and discover it wasn't enough.

Let's imagine how this plays out in the real world. In college, it might be partying too hard the night before a big test. This way, if you get a bad grade, it's because you were hungover, not because you aren't smart enough. As a parent, it might be avoiding a difficult conversation with your daughter about her behavior then later saying, "Well, I didn't want to make things worse." This excuse lets you hide behind the idea that you're doing the best thing for your daughter while avoiding the possibility that you don't know how to handle a situation with your own child (welcome to much of parenthood). Or it might look like not asking for feedback after wrapping up a major work project. You tell yourself, "If there were serious problems, someone would've said something," but underneath that is a fear of hearing something that challenges your self-image as a strong performer.

Whether we come up with an excuse in the moment of disappointment or before to avoid it, we are pulling back from the game. We are retreating to the false sense of safety that is never trying, never going after things that matter to us. We are, one tiny excuse at a time, stepping back from the main stage and joining the critics, the judges, the chattering class of those who lack the courage to get in the arena and instead distract themselves by judging those who do. We are volunteering to sit on the sidelines—*of our own lives*.

From Excuses to Solutions

A few years ago, I was talking with a high school soccer coach in Los Angeles. Just before the season began, she was told the soccer field needed structural repairs and would be shut down for the entire season.

SOLUTIONS: ESCAPING THE EXCUSE TRAP

No field meant no place to practice or play. The coach had a choice: find an alternative or break her players' hearts with a canceled season. She wasn't about to let her girls down.

The school didn't have the budget for an off-site rental, nor did it make sense for the players to contend with rush-hour Los Angeles traffic to practice at a free field elsewhere. So she got creative. One day after school, she walked me to the parking lot. There, on the asphalt, she herself had painted lines to mirror a soccer field. By the time soccer practice rolled around, the parking lot would be clear. The girls would head out to their makeshift "field" and carry on—with the motto their coach had put in their minds on loop: *Where we practice doesn't matter, how we practice does.* There was no time for self-pity, there was only time for performance.

I was struck not just by the coach's ingenuity but also by her refusal to let circumstances set a limit. She didn't complain. She didn't reach for an excuse. She took action, and she searched for a solution. Because of it, her team still got to have a season.

They also got a surprise. Curious how things turned out, I checked in with the coach a few months later. For the first time, her team had won the league championship. Throughout the season, the players kept commenting that the games felt easier. Their theory? Grass blunts the ball's speed. Asphalt doesn't. Practicing on the parking lot had forced the girls to move faster, sharpen their reflexes, and build agility under tougher conditions. So when they hit the grass, the game felt slower—because it was. What was meant as a workaround had become a competitive edge that boosted their performance.

The moral of this story is not to move all grass-based sports practices to asphalt! Injuries will inevitably abound. The moral is that avoiding excuses doesn't just keep you in the game—sometimes literally—but it also guarantees growth, sometimes in ways you never anticipated.

The coach didn't just find a solution. She modeled a mindset, as exemplified in the team's motto. Her players saw firsthand what it looks like when someone hits a wall and looks for where to build a door. And the team didn't just adapt; they excelled.

That's the power of a solution orientation. It's not just about solving the problem in front of you. It's about training your brain to see a limitation and look for leverage. And when that becomes your habit, your default pattern, you put yourself back in the game.

Psychologist Mihaly Csikszentmihalyi is best known for his research on *flow*, a psychological state of deep focus and immersion in an activity, where a person is fully engaged, loses track of time, and performs at his or her best with a sense of effortlessness and satisfaction. In his 1990 book *Flow: The Psychology of Optimal Experience*, he describes "problem-solving ability" as a core characteristic of people who consistently find themselves in high-performance states, or flow.[6] People with high problem-solving ability view problems as puzzles to be solved, not barriers to be resented. And when one develops a pattern of problem-solving, one can more readily enter flow state. From there, the benefits multiply: Technical mastery, of any discipline in question, improves. Focus and strategic thinking get a boost. Productivity and efficiency go up. Resilience and creativity expand. And, critically, confidence sees gains, which makes people even more likely to seek out new challenges and problems to be solved, unleashing a virtuous cycle of growth and improvement.

> **People with high problem-solving ability view problems as puzzles to be solved, not barriers to be resented.**

As if that weren't enough, a solution orientation alone is enough to short-circuit excuses. Why? Because excuses can't survive the creativity and determination of the problem-solving mindset. When excuses say, "This can't be done," solutions storm in to say, "We're going to figure out how this can be done."

If excuses are a performance killer, solutions are excuse killers. When we habitually respond to setbacks with creative effort rather than retreat, we condition ourselves to stay in motion—even when it's hard. *Especially* when it's hard.

Reasons are Real. Excuses are Optional. Motion is Mandatory.

Any honest conversation about excuses must acknowledge that sometimes we have legitimate reasons for a lack of achievement. Life can throw real obstacles in our path—physical, mental, circumstantial. What matters is what we do next.

Remember the Wonderlic from Chapter 1? At one conference, after asking audience members to share why they didn't do as well as they'd expected, a man raised his hand and said, "I'm dyslexic. There's no way I could finish that in twelve minutes." He wasn't blaming anyone or looking for sympathy. He was being honest. His was not an excuse, it was a reason.

But here's what sets top performers apart—they don't let reasons spiral into excuses. They acknowledge their reality, then they get to work anyway.

We all have barriers, some visible, some hidden. But if you allow those barriers to quietly pull you further from your goals, if they start to thwart your effort or define your identity, then you're no longer dealing with a reason. You're dealing with an excuse. And high performers draw that line with conviction.

Few people embody this more clearly than Bethany Hamilton, the professional surfer who lost her arm in a shark attack at age thirteen. After this horrific event, every single person in Hamilton's life would likely have supported her decision to quit surfing. In fact, I'd wager that just about everyone in her life never considered any other option.

Not Bethany. She returned to surfing just *one month* later and, within two years, won a national title. Through determination, faith, and an unwavering commitment to adapt, she re-learned how to paddle and balance on the board with one arm. In the years since, she's competed professionally, raised a family, written books, and built a platform encouraging others to do the same: face the barrier and move past it.

In her blog post "Limitations Aren't Excuses," Bethany writes: "We all have limitations. That's part of being human. The difference is that some people use them as excuses, while others push on…In fact, many people take their limitations and turn them into motivation."[7]

What she faced wasn't a minor challenge—it was a life-altering trauma. And yet, Hamilton refuses to use the word "can't." Not because she denies her reality, but because she refuses to let it define her possibility.

"Not limiting myself," she writes, "means I have given myself permission again and again to try the hard things, listen to my passion, and chase after what really excites me. I can't encourage you enough to just plain be willing to try something hard instead of saying I can't without even trying."

Bethany Hamilton, against the odds, chose the arena—scarred, one-armed, and undeterred.

So the question comes back to you: What's your excuse?

Becoming a Problem Solver

Christian McCaffrey is an elite NFL running back known for his rare combination of speed, agility, and versatility. He's widely known as one of the league's most formidable offensive weapons—a reputation shaped in part through his work with Brian Kula, a world-renowned expert on speed and agility who's coached Olympians and elite athletes alike.

SOLUTIONS: ESCAPING THE EXCUSE TRAP

Kula and I both live in Denver, and we've crossed paths over the years. Recently, I asked him for his thoughts on what separates good from great performers. "It's simple," he said. "Great performers never have excuses as to why they can't get to the gym. When you don't train consistently, you don't play well, and that's not an option for elite performers. So they write a contract with themselves that they will show up for every practice, every training session. And they honor that contract, no matter what. If they're traveling, they find a way to train on the road. If something interferes with their typical training schedule, they rework it to get to the gym anyway. There simply are no excuses."

Here's the thing about a solution mindset—it isn't just an attitude. It's a muscle. That means you don't have to come up with a brilliant fix on day one. You just have to start working it. You wouldn't step into a weight room for the first time and expect to lift what a seasoned athlete lifts. You start with what you can carry. You train with consistency. You get stronger. That's how muscles work. And that's how a solution-orientation works, too.

To start, make a contract with yourself stating that you will no longer be a person who makes excuses. Instead, you are a person who adheres to the belief that solving the problem is more important than avoiding discomfort. By definition, you accept that you can and will tolerate moments of tension between your standards and your performance and choose to stay in the metaphorical arena anyway, while you look for solutions in search of growth.

At first, the pull of the excuse will be strong—you are breaking a habit of reconciling cognitive dissonance to protect your self-image. You resist because you know this is a pitfall of low performance. You know all it does is preserve stasis and prevent improvement. And you're a top performer now. So instead of giving into an easy excuse, the easy out, the moment you feel that familiar story coming on—*it's too late, it won't work, I don't really care that much anyway*—you pause. And then you pivot. You don't need the perfect answer. You just need a better question:

- What's still possible here?
- What haven't I tried yet?
- Who could help me think differently about this?
- What have I failed to consider?

The shift is subtle but profound. Questions like these neutralize excuses. They replace resignation with motion. They turn fear into curiosity. And over time, asking becomes reflex. Then it becomes action. Then it becomes identity.

Before long, you'll notice a change. Problems don't scare you off. Setbacks don't stall you out. You start moving faster, thinking sharper, stretching further. Because you're not circling the problem anymore—you're solving it.

That's when the real transformation happens. You stop seeing yourself as someone who explains *why* things didn't work out, and you start seeing yourself as someone who *makes* things work.

That's the pattern.

That's the muscle.

That's you, in the arena. Ready to try, fail, learn, and try again—no excuses.

CHAPTER 4

Self-Confrontation: Self-Deceptions that Hold Us Back

TOP-PERFORMANCE PATTERNS

Ownership   Solutions   **Self-Confrontation**   Grit

To David, the day started like any other. He got up, drove to his first job site, and sprayed for rodents and roaches. Then the next house. Spray. Next. Spray. Next. On and on until his shift ended.

Then came the usual routine. He drove to get a chocolate milkshake. Then crossed the street to the 7-Eleven for a box of mini doughnuts. Whatever he didn't finish in the car, he finished at home, slumped on the couch, eyes on the TV. Rinse. Repeat. Day after day.

But this day was different.

Flipping through channels, searching for distraction, he landed on something unexpected—a documentary about Navy SEALs. Something about it struck a chord. He stood up, walked into the bathroom, and looked in the mirror.

"You're fat. You're lazy. You're dumb. And no one's coming to save you."

David's path to this moment was not an easy one. From the outside, his flailing life might have seemed inevitable, even understandable. He was born in 1975 in Buffalo, New York, into what he later called "hell on earth." His father—who owned and operated a roller-skating rink by day and was involved in prostitution by night—was violently abusive, physically and emotionally. David, his brother, and their mother endured beatings and terror on a daily basis. He often watched his father brutalize his mom and felt paralyzed with guilt for not being able to protect her.

Eventually, his mother fled with the boys to Brazil, Indiana to live with her parents. But the trauma followed, and new stressors piled on. He struggled in school—undiagnosed learning disabilities, a stutter, a nervous system stuck in fight or flight, and an entrenching belief he was stupid. His environment didn't help: Brazil had a strong Ku Klux Klan presence, and David and his family were one of the few black families in the small town. The racism he faced was constant and dehumanizing.

He scraped through high school, barely graduating. Cheating was the only strategy he knew to avoid failure. Every now and then, ambition would spark—*Maybe you **could** be something*. But the louder voice would always prevail: *Don't be stupid. You're not smart enough. You're not good enough. You don't belong with the people who have goals. You're not one of them, you're nobody.*

Still, on occasion, he could find the wherewithal to try. He attempted to enter the Air Force Pararescue program. He failed the entrance exam once, barely passed it the second time. He was accepted. But, by then, food had become his armor. His weight and various health complications made the training feel impossible. David was right. He couldn't hack it. He didn't deserve to excel, that voice said, victorious again. So he took the job he believed he deserved—spraying for pests at $1,000

SELF-CONFRONTATION: SELF-DECEPTIONS THAT HOLD US BACK

a month while paying $810 in rent. The math wasn't working, and neither was his life. The stress and trauma, the debt, the hopelessness, it all piled higher.

And then came that mirror.

By then, David was 300 pounds and spiraling. But something about that Navy SEALs documentary cut through the noise. Something in it reminded him he was still alive—and maybe, somewhere buried under all the pain, still capable.

"You're out of shape. You're a liar. And you're not going anywhere unless you start being honest about who you are."

This wasn't a pep talk. It was a confrontation. It wasn't David vs. the world anymore. It was David vs. David.

———

That man is David Goggins. Today, he's known around the world as one of the toughest people alive—a retired Navy SEAL with a storied military career that includes combat deployments in Iraq and Afghanistan, as well as service as an Army Ranger and Air Force Tactical Air Controller. But it's not just his war record that made him a legend. Goggins has completed more than sixty ultramarathons, triathlons, and ultra-triathlons—many under extreme physical duress, including one 100-mile race completed with broken feet. He once held the Guinness World Record for most pull-ups in twenty-four hours. He's a best-selling author, a sought-after speaker, and the ultimate symbol of mental fortitude. But above all, he is known for his abiding belief: that we all are capable of far more than we think—*if* we're willing to stop lying to ourselves.

That night in front of the mirror marked the end of Goggins' self-deception. His transformation took time and dogged commitment. It also took finally shedding the story he was telling himself. The lies that he wasn't worthy of success or achievement. The lies that were the very thing standing between him and top performance—even just better performance.

And it started with confronting the truth. The brutal, unvarnished, no-holds-barred truth.

Two Sides of Self-Deception, Same Result

Self-deception is the act of lying to yourself in order to avoid something you don't want to see. It distorts your internal narrative in an attempt to avoid pain, fear, or uncertainty. It goes far beyond denial. It's a form of ego preservation and self-protection.

Self-deception has two faces. Sometimes it looks like self-aggrandizement, where we tell ourselves (and often others) we're better than we are. This is the more obvious version of self-deception. It takes the form of an inflated ego, overconfidence, or arrogance. It's the manager who thinks she doesn't need feedback. Or the athlete who believes he doesn't need to continue to practice the fundamentals. It's the leader who takes all the credit and gives none to the team. Or it's the parent who won't apologize for an overreaction.

In psychology, this is linked to what's known as the *overconfidence effect*—a cognitive bias where people's subjective confidence in their performance far exceeds their actual performance. This tendency isn't just annoying; it's also costly. Overconfident individuals take unnecessary risks, ignore warning signs, and fail to prepare adequately for challenges they think they're already equipped to handle. Not surprisingly, they also prevent their own growth.

In military history, this pitfall has a name: *victory disease*. Napoleon Bonaparte is one of the most infamous faces of this affliction. After a string of decisive victories that earned him a reputation as a military genius, Napoleon began to believe in his own invincibility. This overconfidence drove his invasion of Russia in 1812, a notoriously catastrophic decision. He underestimated the harshness of the Russian winter, overextended his supply lines, and assumed victory would be easy and swift. What followed was a disastrous retreat and staggering death. His Grand Armée went from 600,000 to 100,000 soldiers. It marked the beginning of his downfall. The man once known for his strategic brilliance fell prey to self-deception. He believed he couldn't lose for no reason other than he hadn't.

The other face of self-deception is quieter, the David Goggins kind. It looks like self-loathing and lowered self-expectations. It's the kind where we tell ourselves we are incapable of excellence or achievement. It's something far more insidious than giving up. It removes any reason to bother trying. It goes to dramatic lengths, sometimes through outright degrading and abusive self-talk, to avoid the possibility of giving up.

In its milder forms, this face of self-deception can be mistaken for humility or realism. But it's not. Because it's rooted in lies, not reality. It's just as delusional as the self-enhancing, overconfident kind, and it's still a way of protecting the ego—just in reverse. If you convince yourself you can't win, you don't have to risk losing. If you say the opportunity wasn't right for you anyway, you don't have to admit you were afraid to take it.

Self-aggrandizement says, "I'm chosen. I'm naturally gifted. I don't need to try." Self-loathing says, "Achievement is for other people. I'm not that person. There's no need to try." Two faces, same outcome: low performance. Or worse still, no performance.

The Psychology of Self-Deception

Self-deception is a particularly fascinating pitfall of low performance. The evolutionary logic behind self-enhancing deception is relatively straightforward. To gain or maintain status within a group, we need others to perceive us as capable, competent, and worthy. When we don't fully believe we are, we look for ways to convince ourselves otherwise—so we can then project that belief outward. Biologist Robert Trivers and evolutionary psychologist William von Hippel have long studied this behavior and landed on a simple explanation for some rather sophisticated mental gymnastics: We deceive ourselves to better deceive others. If we truly believe the lie, then it's no longer a lie when we say it. On a subconscious level, we convert the lie into a "truth," making it easier to broadcast with conviction and secure the social approval we seek.[1]

But why would people deceive themselves into believing they're *less* capable than they really are? Wouldn't this reduce their perceived value to the tribe and increase their risk of exclusion?

Trivers and von Hippel suggest that this "downward" self-deception is often learned. When people, especially as children, receive repeated messages from authority figures that they are less capable, worthy, or valuable than they are, they may internalize this false narrative and develop a *self-diminishment bias*.[2] Over time, it becomes adaptive: shrinking the self to avoid conflict, appease the aggressor, or reduce the likelihood of further harm. This form of under-confidence can smooth interpersonal dynamics, particularly in volatile environments. It signals submission, validates the superiority of the dominant party, and minimizes perceived threat.

This is exactly what David Goggins did. His home and school life bombarded him with the same message: you're stupid, bad, unworthy. He learned to shrink—to keep his self-belief small as a way of staying safe in a life that constantly threatened him. Accepting the lies others told reduced cognitive dissonance, thereby giving him some sense of control. To believe he was worthless was to stabilize an otherwise chaotic reality. In evolutionary terms, this self-deception served a purpose: If he accepted his low place in the social order, he could avoid provoking further attacks. Better to preserve a meager standing than to reach for more, fail visibly, and risk losing everything.

Goggins represents a dramatic example. Many of us self-diminish for reasons that aren't born of childhood trauma. Often we do this simply to avoid an undesirable outcome or stressful reaction. We've all seen moments—or lived them—when playing small offers a short-term benefit. Think of deflecting credit in front of a power-hungry boss to avoid retaliation. Or letting a loud colleague dominate a meeting to keep the peace. These acts of self-suppression can feel strategic in the moment, but over time they chip away at our performance and limit our potential. The longer we deceive ourselves into thinking it's OK not to claim what's ours, the more likely we are to act accordingly.

Whether it takes the form of self-enhancement or self-diminishment, self-deception guarantees low performance for the same core reason: It severs our connection to reality and gets us off the hook. Self-enhancement is the ego's con—it lets us fake greatness and skip the grind, but it robs us of growth. Self-diminishment is the coward's lie—it lets us play small and quit early, but it kills any shot at becoming something more. In both cases, we cut ourselves off from accurate self-assessment. And without it, there can be no meaningful progress.

High performance doesn't begin with motivation. It begins with coming to grips with reality—about who you are, where you are, and what it will take to become something more.

Confronting the Cold, Hard Truth

Early in my career, I taught social studies at a high school in Bermuda. I had just completed teaching a World History unit and, while I don't want to brag, I crushed it. It wasn't just a day or two of feeling locked in, with my students totally engrossed. It was day after day, week after week, for the whole unit. I would end each class thinking, *I'm making such an impact. The kids are so engaged. We're killing it.*

Then came the unit test.

I went into the day with total confidence that the kids were going to kick ass on the test. And why not? I had kicked ass on teaching them. But across the board, the scores were poor. Even my top students struggled. *Oof,* was it a gut punch.

Fortunately, I'd been mentored by some exceptional educators—teachers who drilled into my brain that great teachers are those who take responsibility for the outcomes of their instruction. In fact, owning the outcomes of one's teaching is a prerequisite of becoming a great teacher. I could feel the pull to blame the test, the students, or anything that would preserve the lie that my instruction had been flawless. But that was just the ego going into self-preservation mode. The reality was clear: I hadn't done my job well enough.

I had to get real, get honest, and get back on track. When I forced myself to analyze what went wrong, the problem stood out. I had over-indexed on keeping students engaged and under-indexed on helping them internalize the key concepts they'd need to know for the test. Engagement is critical, but it's only half the job. The other half is ensuring students understand what they need to know. In chasing engagement, I had let them down. As it turned out, I didn't crush it. I sacrificed academic outcomes at the altar of *feeling* like a great teacher instead of *being* a great teacher.

After confronting the truth, I shared it with my students. I told them the results weren't their fault—they were mine. I hadn't done enough to set them up for success. And I would do better. Bruised but determined to improve, I overhauled my instructional plan for the next unit. I baked in more intentional reinforcement, a different mix of instructional strategies that I thought would lead students to the right place, and more repetition. In committing to my own performance, I enabled the students to commit to theirs. On their next test, overall scores improved twenty percent.

I'll be honest: When I first thought about the pattern that opposes the self-deception pitfall, I landed on self-awareness. It made sense. But something about it didn't sit right. It was too broad. Too soft. When I

SELF-CONFRONTATION: SELF-DECEPTIONS THAT HOLD US BACK

came across the phrase "self-confrontation," I knew I'd found what we needed.

Self-awareness is essential. You can't build healthy relationships—especially with yourself—without it. You can't grow or self-actualize without it. I'm all in on cultivating awareness. Please do it. You'll be better for it.

But self-awareness casts a wide net. It includes everything from realizing you're talking too much in a meeting to recognizing you just hit someone with your backpack while boarding a plane. And while it encompasses recognizing the lies we tell ourselves, self-awareness simply alerts us to them.

> Self-deception is a stubborn beast. It's not born just from a lack of awareness; it's a lie we've gone to great subconscious lengths to turn into a "truth."

Self-deception is a stubborn beast. It's not born just from a lack of awareness; it's a lie we've gone to great subconscious lengths to turn into a "truth." To root it out, we need something more exacting than self-awareness to take it on. We need something up to the task. Something with teeth. That thing is self-confrontation. It's Goggins looking in the mirror: "You're out of shape. You're a liar. And you're not going anywhere unless you start being honest about who you are."

Self-confrontation is not about self-punishment or wallowing in failure. It's about facing hard truths head-on, often the ones we want to avoid the most. It's what happens when we recognize we've been lying to ourselves—either by inflating our abilities or shrinking them—and then choosing to name it, examine it, and replace it with something honest. While the term "self-confrontation" appears in both therapeutic and religious contexts, here we're using it to describe the act of directly facing the internal narratives that block performance or progress in any context. It's a deliberate decision to interrogate your story and rewrite a new one—one rooted in reality, the present, and what we can control, and one oriented toward growth.

Psychologists have studied this concept under various names and methods, but the takeaway is consistent: When people confront themselves honestly and directly, the fog of self-deception begins to clear. Self-assessment becomes more accurate. Motivation sharpens. And performance can finally improve.

One route to self-confrontation is *metacognitive reflection*, a practice commonly used in education. The teachers among us are familiar with metacognitive strategies—those strategies students use to think about their own thinking, such as planning, monitoring, and evaluating how they learn. For example, a student might set a goal before reading ("I will identify three main themes"), or pause during a math problem to ask, "Does this step make sense?" Research consistently shows that these strategies improve self-direction, adaptability, and achievement.

Metacognitive reflection has also been widely studied in professional environments. Research from Harvard Business School found that employees who engaged in structured reflection after tasks, such as analyzing their decision-making processes and assumptions, showed significantly greater performance improvement over time compared to those who did not reflect.[3] Several such studies reinforce that metacognitive strategies can sharpen judgment, reduce cognitive bias, and facilitate the kind of honest self-appraisal that disrupts self-deception and supports meaningful improvement.

Another related practice is *performance feedback review*, used frequently in sports. Athletes watch video footage of their performance to analyze not how they remember it or wish it had been, but what actually took place. They're forced to confront gaps between effort and execution, between story and reality. And that gap is where growth lives.

In cognitive behavioral therapy (CBT), something similar happens

SELF-CONFRONTATION: SELF-DECEPTIONS THAT HOLD US BACK

through intentional questioning. CBT is a widely used, evidence-based approach that helps people challenge distorted beliefs to improve behavior and emotional health. One tool used in CBT is *thought disputation*, where the client identifies a recurring, unhelpful belief ("I always mess things up"), traces where it came from, and examines whether it still holds up under scrutiny. In essence, it's an internal cross-examination in which a person seeks evidence to dispute the belief. The goal is to get honest so better choices can emerge.

All these techniques share a core strength: They help people create just enough distance from themselves to see things more clearly. This concept of *objective self-awareness* dates back to a 1972 theory from psychologists Robert Wicklund and Shelley Duval (not to be confused with Shelley Duvall of *Popeye* fame).[4] They suggest that when people see themselves as "objects" in the environment slightly beyond the one they're in—like in a mirror or on video—they begin comparing their actual behavior to their internal standards, such as personal values or goals. This spotlight on the gap between self-perception and reality can be deeply uncomfortable, but also transformative. While later research challenged some aspects of Wickland and Duval's model, the underlying insight has held up: Creating even a moment of psychological distance can make self-evaluation more honest and productive.

Call it metacognitive reflection, performance feedback review, or disputing thoughts—the goal is the same: to establish enough mental distance to examine your story with objectivity and clarity. Self-confrontation requires perspective. It's not just noticing what you're doing. The goal of self-confrontation is to step outside yourself just enough to say, "That's not true. That's not helping. That has to change."

It's not always comfortable, and it's not always instant. But it works. And it's a pattern that top performers use all the time—so much so that they report it gets easier, reflexive, and eventually even welcome and wanted. When you build the muscle of self-confrontation, you gain access to reality. And that's where better performance begins—not with over-hyped or lowered self-expectations, but with truth.

After all, how can you improve tomorrow if you're dishonest about where you are today?

Ways to Self-Confront—With Care

Self-confrontation can be transformative—but it can also be difficult, even painful. Sometimes our self-deception runs deep, reaching all the way back to formative or unhealed moments from our past. If that's true for you, you don't have to go it alone.

It's normal for self-confrontation to stir discomfort–even guilt or anger. Often, that discomfort is productive and a necessary part of the process. But if your self-work brings up recurring pain, flashbacks, or persistent self-loathing, it may be time to seek help. Trusted therapists, coaches, or mentors can help you navigate the tension safely. Seeking guidance doesn't mean you're weak. On the contrary, it takes courage to know when something's too heavy to carry alone and to ask for help. Working with an objective third party can often accelerate the kind of objective self-awareness we're trying to cultivate.

That said, many of the lies we tell ourselves—the half-truths, the ego-fed rationalizations—can be addressed with simple, evidence-informed techniques you can practice on your own, like reflecting, journaling, or mirror meditation (a research-based method of speaking directly, compassionately, and candidly to yourself in the mirror, which creates enough distance to reduce self-criticism, foster self-compassion, and motivate behavior change).[5] These approaches are especially helpful when your self-deception is tied to performance in a specific domain rather than broader, more existential questions.

SELF-CONFRONTATION: SELF-DECEPTIONS THAT HOLD US BACK

Self-deception is sneaky because it is a kind of defense. It often forms when we're trying to shield ourselves from pain, fear, or failure. It's this reason that makes it so difficult to cut through the lies—for so long, we have believed they protected us. And in certain past circumstances, they actually might have protected us.

But we buy the lie at our peril. This is especially true when the lie is rooted in the past and no longer pertains to our present. No matter how adaptive, even wise a self-deception might have been the first time you used it, it will eventually outlive its purpose and inevitably begin to stand in your way. It will eventually keep you from achieving the goals that mean the most to you. And when your self-deception makes you feel categorically unworthy or superior, then it will keep you from *you*.

When self-confrontation is practiced with care and intention, it isn't harsh or punishing—it's liberating. It allows you to identify what's holding you back and reclaim what's possible. Because the truth—when faced with candor and courage—doesn't shrink us. It sets us free.

Let's Take a Page from Goggins

I mean this almost literally.

In 2018, David Goggins published his memoir, *Can't Hurt Me: Master Your Mind and Defy the Odds*. Four years later, he followed up with *Never Finished: Unshackle Your Mind and Win the War Within*. In both, you'll find a man who is anything but typical. Goggins pushes himself far beyond any reasonable limit—running on broken bones, training through illness, enduring pain most of us would never invite. And then, once healed, he finds some new (often literal!) bleeding edge to push past. He calls himself a "lab rat"—a human experiment designed to test the lengths that sheer willpower can take a human.

In his books and interviews, he's consistent and clear: He's not asking anyone else to live like him. He doesn't glorify suffering for its own sake. In fact, he reminds us often—*you don't need to be me, and most would never want to be me.* The point isn't *what* he achieves. The point is *that* he achieves. It's that if someone with his past—raised in chaos, shaped by trauma, haunted by self-deception for decades—can forge a life of discipline and peak performance, then transformation isn't reserved for the lucky or the gifted. It's available to anyone willing to get real.

So let's take *that* page from Goggins. You don't need to become him. You don't need to run ultramarathons or shatter records. But you can use him as proof. Proof that the lies you tell yourself are not permanent. That the story can be changed. That performance can evolve.

You can look in the mirror—literal or metaphorical—get honest and choose to live by lies no more. In fact, *you have to* if you want to do great things.

Self-deception says it's you against the world. When you play this game, the world will always win.

Self-confrontation sets you straight: It's you vs. you. Now when you play *that* game, anything is possible.

CHAPTER 5

Grit: Resisting the Pull to Give Up

TOP-PERFORMANCE PATTERNS

Ownership   Solutions   Self-Confrontation   **Grit**

The sun is high and punishing. After a sustained and stressful drought and then days of rain, the sky has cleared, and now it blazes. His mouth is dry. His legs ache. He's been walking for hours, and the signs of dehydration—accumulated over days of water rationing—are taking hold. But he cannot stop. Somewhere ahead, at a bend in the creek, clean water awaits. His survival depends on reaching it, and so does his tribe's.

To turn back now guarantees death, whereas pressing on gives him a chance. So he walks. And walks. And walks—until he finally reaches the creek and drinks like his life depends on it. Because it does. With his strength partly restored, he fills clay pots and begins the long journey back. When he arrives at camp, he collapses from exhaustion. His job is done. For now, he can give in to rest. It's someone else's turn to carry the load.

Centuries later, under a similarly punishing sun, another young man walked. And walked. And walked. Xavier had someplace important to be—his eighth-grade graduation. But his grandfather's car had broken down, and there was no backup plan. So he started walking. Six miles, in the St. Louis, Missouri, summer heat.

The sun was getting to him. He had no water. He was so thirsty he thought about turning back. But he couldn't give up. He believed this ceremony wasn't optional. It was the required gateway to a better life, a signifier of his effort, and permission to keep striving for more. So he asked a stranger for a dollar, bought a water, and pressed on. He arrived, exhausted but triumphant. The walk was over. The seat was earned. He could let it support him as he relaxed and enjoyed the fruits of his labor—not just of the day, but of his academic career to date and the future he wants, now in even closer view.

These two humans' worlds couldn't be more different. One fought to survive; the other to thrive. But the principle is the same. Tens of thousands of years ago, most of our stressors threatened our physical survival. Today, most of our stressors threaten our ability to grow, advance, and build meaningful, self-sufficient lives. Our nervous systems don't always know the difference. Both feel existential. Both demand effort. And in both cases, giving up is the easy option—but not the one that leads anywhere worth going.

> Giving up is the easy option—but not the one that leads anywhere worth going.

What It Means to Give Up

Giving up isn't always obvious to the observer. Sometimes it's loud—a declaration, a dropped ball, a dramatic exit. But more often, it's quiet. Subtle. Internal. It's an unspoken decision to cease effort—even if the effort appears to persist.

At its core, giving up is the act of forfeiting one's effort or intention in the face of discomfort, uncertainty, or difficulty. It's choosing comfort at the expense of the climb. And this choice doesn't always happen in full view. When I keynote, an audience member may stop putting any thought into the Wonderlic and mindlessly fill out every question. An athlete may finish the game but stop trying to win. A leader may keep attending meetings but give up on driving change. A parent may stop initiating conversations with his teenager, not out of indifference, but because trying feels hard and futile. The outer performance can continue, but the inner drive does not. You can still show up and simply go through the motions. Or giving up can look like full-fledged disengagement, where you quit completely or don't show up at all.

No matter how it looks and who can see it, giving up is, arguably, the ultimate pitfall. The earlier pitfalls in this book—blame, excuses, and self-deception—can all make giving up more likely. They are certainly a step in giving-up's direction. We might blame others to justify stopping. We might make excuses to soften the shame of retreat. We might convince ourselves we never really wanted the goal in the first place. These are defense mechanisms and delays. But, on their own, they lack the finality of giving up. After applying one of these pitfalls to interrupt our effort, we still have to make the decision to cease effort entirely.

Furthermore, blame, excuses, and self-deception are not always a precursor to giving up. Giving up can happen all on its own—slowly, subtly, or all at once.

To be clear, the decision to quit something isn't always wrong. There's a time to walk away—when the cost outweighs the benefit, when persistence means real risks to yourself or others, or when circumstances change such that the mission no longer makes sense. But that's not what we're talking about here. We're talking about the kind of giving up that occurs because we've hit resistance and don't want to push through. We're talking about disengaging from what we still care about just because it got hard.

The Psychology of Giving Up

When you stop to think about it, it's strange how easily we give up on things that do matter to us. Every one of us knows how good it feels to push through something hard and come out the other side. It's a double win: We get the thing we wanted, and we gain the deeper satisfaction of proving to ourselves that we can stretch, grow, and do hard things. In fact, it's the difficulty itself that gives the achievement its weight. If it were easy, it wouldn't feel like much of an achievement at all.

If we know how good it feels to persevere and achieve, why isn't that feeling enough to motivate us through the challenging moments? Why are we so often quick to pack it in?

Enter, once again, our ancient wiring.

As odd as it sounds, we're biologically wired to give up—when it serves our survival. Our ancestors had to be careful about when and how they exerted energy. In a world where food was scarce and predators could be lurking behind any bend, unnecessary exertion could cost you your life. Evolution rewarded those who conserved energy, avoided risk, and opted for the path of least resistance whenever possible.

Think of our early ancestor trekking miles in scorching heat to reach water and return it to his tribe. Once he completed his task, he *had* to rest. His brain and body were alerting him to go into self-protection mode. To immediately head out again would've been dangerous, maybe even fatal. He needed to conserve energy in case another threat appeared. And the tribe needed him alive. Rest wasn't laziness, it was survival.

But what once kept us alive is now starkly out of sync with our modern reality. Most of us will never go truly hungry, at least not for long. Calories are everywhere. So is climate control. We can avoid heat and cold with the press of a button. Most of us will only encounter predatory animals behind thick Plexi-glass at a zoo. Energy and calorie preservation in the name of preparedness for the next threat is rarely needed in our modern lives. Yet our brains still respond to challenges as though they pose a serious threat. And our brains still send the same ancient signals: *Stop. Save energy. Play it safe.*

This wiring doesn't just apply to physical effort. It applies to mental strain as well. Cognitive work burns energy, too, and our brains are constantly scanning for ways to conserve it. It is for this reason that when we go into fight or flight mode, our vision narrows, our thinking simplifies, and our focus becomes reactive and survival-driven. In high-stakes moments, the brain deprioritizes complex thinking in favor of quick, decisive action. This was helpful when having to make a snap decision to dodge a predator. It's less helpful when trying to finish a dissertation, launch a business, or stay present in a difficult conversation.

Modern neuroscience confirms this instinct: The brain treats effort as a cost. In the early 2010s, neuroscientist Matthew Botvinick, along with collaborators Amitai Shenhav and Jonathan Cohen, integrated research from psychology, behavioral economics, and neuroscience into a unified model of how we regulate cognitive effort. Up to that point, most research on executive function—which includes mental skills like focus, planning, impulse control, and working memory—had been the domain of cognitive psychology and behavioral studies. But with advances in fMRI (functional magnetic resonance imaging) technology, researchers could begin observing how the brain allocates effort in real time by tracking blood flow to different brain regions.

This model crystallized into the researchers' formal theory, the *Expected Value of Control*, where Botvinick and his team defined "control" as the mental energy we use to stay focused, resist distraction, and pursue a goal when the easy route would be to give up.[1] It's not just deliberate cognitive effort; it's also the decision to sustain that effort even when it becomes uncomfortable. Drawing from both original fMRI studies and a synthesis of existing research, Botvinick and his team proposed that effort isn't allocated purely based on willpower or some generalized motivation. Instead, their theory suggests that, when facing a task, the brain performs a kind of internal cost-benefit analysis. It calculates the expected value of exerting control in any given moment. If the expected payoff isn't high enough to justify the strain, the brain pulls back.

The theory of *ego depletion*—the idea that self-control wears down like a muscle—adds another layer to this picture. As we resist distractions, manage emotions, or persist through hard tasks, we gradually drain our mental energy. And when our energy is low, even simple effort can feel overwhelming. What the *Expected Value of Control* model helps explain is *why* ego depletion leads to disengagement: As our fatigue increases, the perceived cost of effort goes up, making even meaningful goals seem not worth the strain. The result? We check out, not because we've stopped caring, but because effort now feels too expensive to spend.

This research points to a protective system designed to conserve energy, which made sense back in a world where life required more physical effort than complex cognitive effort to survive. But in today's world, where progress often demands sustained and complex thinking, this ancient wiring can hold us back and even compel us to give up.

Today, we give up more for psychological reasons, but the instinct is the same. We retreat to avoid the pain of failure, which the brain still interprets as a threat—not just to achievement but also to belonging. Deep down, we fear that failure might signal unworthiness, and unworthiness threatens our standing in the group. And, as we well know by now, to lose standing in the tribe was to risk safety and survival. Giving up, then, is perceived as the safer option.

To be a top performer in our modern world, we need something to override our biology when it misreads the situation and incorrectly goes into self-protection mode. We need an antidote to giving up. We need grit.

Failing the Way to Top Performance

In 2012, at age forty-one, Sarah Blakely became the world's youngest self-made billionaire. The venture that got her there? Spanx, the shapewear company she launched just fourteen years earlier.

GRIT: RESISTING THE PULL TO GIVE UP

As Blakely tells it, she quite literally failed her way to the top.[2] She once dreamed of becoming a lawyer, but after failing the LSAT twice, she pivoted. She tried out a few other careers and failed. She took a job selling fax machines—door to door, cold call by cold call. She was routinely kicked out of offices and had phones slammed in her ear. Yet she persisted. After five years and one particularly brutal stretch of rejection, she knew she needed to chart a new path. She became determined to invent something that made people's lives better. Two years later, she had the idea for smoothing, slimming shapewear, born out of a void she noticed in her own wardrobe.

She got to work making prototypes and needed a production partner. She learned that most hosiery mills were based in North Carolina, not far from where she lived in Atlanta. When cold calls failed, she decided to hit the road. Using weekends and vacation days, she drove up to pitch her product in person. Every single mill turned her down. And several mill owners were all too happy to tell her that her product was "dumb" and would never sell. Again and again, she was told "no." So she regrouped and considered her next move. Until one day, a few weeks after meeting Blakely, one mill owner called her back. The owner's daughters, personally familiar with the problem Blakely's product was seeking to solve, had urged him to reconsider. That call became the break that launched a global brand.

Blakely credits her grit and tenacity, and therefore her success, to the best advice she ever got: *Go out and fail.*[3] Every night at dinner, her father would ask her and her brother, "What did you fail at today?" If they had nothing to report, he'd be disappointed. But if one of them said something like, "I tried out for something, and I was awful!," he'd give them a high five. The message was loud and clear, and it stuck: Failure isn't a matter of outcomes. Failure is not trying. Failure is giving up the moment you hit resistance.

Giving up is deeply human. It's biological, neurological, and psychological. But so is grit. The capacity to override that wiring, to push through effort and uncertainty—that's what defines high performers. Not that they never feel like giving up—they absolutely do. But they've built the muscle to keep going when every part of them wants to stop. This potential exists in all of us.

The Power of Grit

Psychologist Angela Duckworth defines grit as "passion and perseverance for long-term goals." Grit is not talent. It's not luck. It's not even raw intelligence or physical ability. Instead, as Duckworth puts it, "grit is about having what some researchers call an 'ultimate concern'—a goal you care about so much that it organizes and gives meaning to almost everything you do. And grit is holding steadfast to that goal. Even when you fall down. Even when you screw up. Even when progress toward that goal is halting or slow."[4]

Duckworth's extensive research on grit was sparked with a simple observation: The most successful people in a wide range of fields weren't necessarily the smartest or most gifted. What else, Duckworth wondered, was driving their success and achievement? When Duckworth stumbled onto an intriguing fact, she conceived the idea for a study to get answers.

Winning admission to West Point is a grueling two-year process, involving applications, physical and cognitive tests, interviews, evaluations, campus visits, nomination, and final review. New cadets must then complete a six-week summer initiation called "Beast Barracks", which is as intense as the name suggests. These soldiers-in-training endure nonstop days that start at 6:00 a.m. sharp and go late into the evenings. They're filled with various drills that push them to their mental, physical, and emotional limits. Duckworth was surprised to learn that 3 out of every 100 cadets quit the program within the first days of Beast Barracks. After making it through such a long and arduous admissions process, what would cause some to bail just days in? This question was at the heart of Duckworth's now-famous longitudinal study of 11,258 West Point cadets.[5]

For the study, Duckworth created the twelve-item Grit Scale that each cadet filled out throughout Beast Barracks. She and her team found that grit was a better indicator than IQ, SAT scores, and physical fitness of which cadets would make it through the six weeks. She saw this pattern repeated with National Spelling Bee finalists, where those with higher grit were more likely to stay committed and sustain effort under pressure.

While her research confirms that there are other factors determinative of achievement, grit is by far the most important when it comes to pushing through the most challenging, exhausting, and discouraging stretches on our path toward a goal. Grit—more than talent, skill, intelligence, and physical ability—is the performance pattern that is up to the task of overpowering the pull to give up.

Other researchers have added important insights to the conversation. Carol Dweck's work on growth mindset complements grit beautifully.[6] A *growth mindset* is the belief that abilities can be developed through effort. By contrast, a *fixed mindset* is the belief that abilities are static and unchangeable through effort. When we believe we can improve, we're more likely to persist. Without that belief, effort feels futile. If effort feels futile, then giving up is taken off the menu. If you can change nothing about your abilities, then you need not try. Talk about a self-defeating external locus of control and our ancient, outdated, ego-preserving wiring run amok.

This is where research from Duckworth and Dweck dovetails. Duckworth has argued that grit and growth mindset work hand in hand: People who believe they can grow are more willing to do the hard work that growth requires. Put another way, a growth mindset is a prerequisite of grit.

Psychologist Albert Bandura's concept of self-efficacy—a strong belief in self—also plays a key role in this context.[7] People with high self-efficacy are more likely to be resilient, persist through challenges, recover from disappointment, and remain engaged in and committed to their interest and activities. Those with low self-efficacy are—you guessed it—more likely to disengage and give up. But when we adopt a growth mindset and apply grit, we can change our self-belief and kick off a virtuous cycle that ultimately boosts our belief in what we're made of, capable of, and determined to achieve.

How to Build Grit

Building grit is not just about endurance. It's also about cultivating belief. And unlike innate intelligence or natural gifts, grit is something we can all get more of. So how do we do it?

One way is to make the stakes personal. In her book, *Grit: The Power of Passion and Perseverance*, Duckworth devotes a chapter to purpose.[8] She explains that, when a goal connects to your values or a sense of purpose larger than yourself, your tolerance for pain increases. She also encourages readers to seek out a role model, someone whose sense of purpose inspires you to connect your goals to purpose in order to fuel your grit. In the absence of such role models, books and documentaries about people who've achieved great things can be excellent, inspiring, and motivating surrogates.

Another way is to focus on progress, not perfection. Show me a person who's achieved something great, and I'll show you a person who's made countless mistakes, encountered all kinds of roadblocks, and considered giving up several times—but chose to persevere regardless. To pursue perfection is to pursue a destination that does not exist. Bluntly, perfection is not a thing. But achievement is. So pursue the path that is real, not the mirage. Embrace the messiness. Do the uncelebrated, unsexy reps—even when no one is watching, *especially* when no one is watching. And regularly take stock not of where you are but how far you've come, as this will fortify your growth mindset and create more grit.

And finally, grit grows in community. We're more likely to persist when we're surrounded by people who normalize struggle and celebrate effort (cue Sarah Blakely's failure-loving father!). If you spend time around people who give up at the first sign of difficulty, that mindset just might seep in. But if you surround yourself with friends and colleagues who reframe failure as feedback, who keep choosing challenge, and who push through resistance in pursuit of real growth, you'll rise with them. Grit is contagious. So is quitting. Choose your influences wisely.

As we set out to build grit, it's important to remember what grit is not. It's not stubbornness. It's not grinding yourself into the ground to prove something that doesn't matter. And it's not clinging to goals that are no longer worth the cost. As we've discussed, there are times when quitting is the right move. But when a goal remains relevant, meaningful, and possible, grit becomes the unlock. It's what enables sustained, focused effort through the inevitable struggles and setbacks on the path to something worth fighting for.

Grit only kicks in when things get hard. If the road is smooth, you don't need it. As Duckworth points out, hardship is not the obstacle to grit. It's the environment that calls it forward.

Root your effort in purpose. Focus on progress. Celebrate growth and wins along the way. Surround yourself with gritty, inspiring people and stories. And when you find yourself in one of those challenging environments, your grit will be at the ready—willing and able to help you push onward, not just because you can but because you *know* the work is worth it.

When Others Tell Us to Give Up

Misty Copeland is one of the most groundbreaking ballet dancers of her generation. In 2015, she made history as the first African American woman to be promoted to principal dancer at the prestigious American

Ballet Theatre—an achievement that ended a seventy-five-year barrier in the company's history. Over her career, she has performed lead roles in iconic productions like *Swan Lake* and *Romeo and Juliet*. In 2014, she was named one of Time's 100 Most Influential People, and her impact has been recognized with honors including the Dance Magazine Award, the Leonore Annenberg Fellowship, and the NAACP Spingarn Medal. All along, she has been an advocate for a more inclusive view of and approach to ballet. And none of this—not her achievements, nor her influence on her field—would have ever happened had she listened to the critics.

Ballet has long favored an exceptionally lean, almost fragile body type—one Copeland never had. Her frame was always more muscular, more athletic. Despite her natural talent, relentless discipline, and clear and consistent upward trajectory, she was repeatedly told she didn't fit the mold. Her body, many would say, would hold her back. She'd never reach the upper echelons of the form. So why keep going?

In interviews and her memoir *Life in Motion*, Copeland emphasizes that grit was always in her bones: "Perseverance has always just been something that was in me. And it was a tool that came in very handy as a ballerina."[9] She often describes how she didn't let rejection break her. Instead, she used it to fuel her. In one recounting, after being told to "lengthen" (a euphemism for losing weight), she fought back—not with denial but with action.[10] She adjusted her training to strengthen her body so her performance could improve and then speak for itself.

When the critics said she didn't belong, she refused to quit. Instead, she chose to let her performance change what "belonging" in ballet meant. When the naysayers' voices got loud, she found even more grit in a sense of purpose—that her success was not her own but a beacon of hope for all the dancers who were told they were in the wrong body type, wrong skin color, or wrong art form altogether.

The pull to give up won't always come from within. But sometimes the critics' chorus can grow loud enough that it begins to crowd out our own voice. Sometimes the critics can make us wonder if we should, in fact, give up. When this happens, remember: The critics sit safely and comfortably on the sidelines and judge those who, unlike themselves, have the courage, the grit, and the confidence to get in the arena and face what comes—bruises, failures, and all.

Grit Pays Us Back in Spades

Our eighth-grade friend from the beginning of this chapter, Xavier, is real, and so is his story. In May 2023, after his grandfather's car broke down, Xavier really did walk six miles in the heat to make it to his graduation. And his grit paid off in more ways than one. He showed up. He got to walk the stage. He got to be celebrated. And he received an opportunity few fourteen-year-olds could dream of.

The ceremony was held at Harris-Stowe State University, a historically black university in St. Louis, Missouri. Among the attendees that day was the university's president, Dr. LaTonia Collins Smith. When word spread about Xavier's long walk, Collins Smith was deeply moved. "He wanted to be present," she said in an interview with the local news. "(That) speaks volumes. Half the battle is showing up."[11]

In that same interview, Xavier explained his decision to walk the six miles: "If you like really want to get something, then you have to work hard for it." Collins Smith recognized in Xavier that telltale grit that separates low performers from high achievers. She met Xavier after the ceremony—and offered him a full-ride scholarship to Harris-Stowe, on the spot. Xavier was thrilled. He thought it meant he would always have a ride to college and never have to walk.

Of course, it meant something far more profound: Doors were opening because Xavier chose not to quit. While Xavier still has time to decide which college to attend, one decision he made long ago continues to shape his future: to keep working hard and excelling in school.

Of his motivation, he says: "It basically comes from who I am, and the kind of person I want to be."

That's the thing about grit. It doesn't just keep you from giving up. It keeps you on the path to becoming who you're meant to be. Grit is a pattern of high performance, yes—but it's also a gravitational force. It propels us forward when everything in us wants to stop. It says, "You *can* keep going," even when your ancient wiring is incorrectly signaling threat. It says, "You *can* do hard things," even when the world tells you otherwise. It says, "This work *still* matters," even when it's painful, thankless, or slow.

> That's the thing about grit. It doesn't just keep you from giving up. It keeps you on the path to becoming who you're meant to be.

And grit doesn't just rescue us from the pitfall of quitting. It weakens the pull of all the others, too. Grit makes excuses harder to tolerate. It makes blame harder to cast onto others. It makes self-deception harder to maintain. When you commit to keep moving toward important goals no matter what, you no longer need the mental gymnastics that come with low performance. You don't have to protect your ego. You don't have to pretend you don't care. You don't have to explain away your lack of effort. You just have to keep showing up and trying.

The more you do that, the more confident you become—not in a puffed-up, hollow way, but in a real, earned way. You begin to trust yourself. To believe you can push through discomfort. To see difficulty not as a stop sign but as a proving ground. And the more grit you use, the more you have. Like a muscle, it strengthens with use. Each time you override your wiring, each time you choose to persist instead of quit, you're not just accomplishing something—you're becoming someone.

Grit changes everything. Not because it makes life easier, but because it makes us stronger. More focused. More capable. More free. And that's the essence of top performance—not raw talent, not perfect conditions, but the practiced pattern of perseverance. The choice to keep walking, even when the road gets hard. Just like Xavier did.

CHAPTER 6

Culture: Building an Ecosystem of Excellence

In his 2007 Berkshire Hathaway shareholder letter, investor and CEO Warren Buffett didn't hide from one of the biggest blunders of his career:

Finally, I made an even worse mistake when I said "yes" to Dexter, a shoe business I bought in 1993 for $433 million in Berkshire stock (25,203 shares of A). What I had assessed as durable competitive advantage vanished within a few years. But that's just the beginning: By using Berkshire stock, I compounded this error hugely. That move made the cost to Berkshire shareholders not $400 million, but rather $3.5 billion. In essence, I gave away 1.6 % of a wonderful business—one now valued at $220 billion—to buy a worthless business.

To date, Dexter is the worst deal that I've made. But I'll make more mistakes in the future—you can bet on that. A line from Bobby Bare's country song explains what too often happens with acquisitions: "I've never gone to bed with an ugly woman, but I've sure woke up with a few."[1]

Paying with stock is risky. It's trading away a slice of future growth for a giant question mark. The only way this kind of investment pays off is if the purchased company is a wild success. That's why Buffett almost never paid with stock. He would only do so if he believed a business was as good or better than Berkshire Hathaway.

Dexter was a Maine-based company that produced all its shoes in the United States. When Buffett made the acquisition in 1993, he missed what was happening on the other side of the globe. Factories in China were beginning to turn out skilled work at a fraction of Maine's wages. In just a few short years, the American market was flooded with overseas competitors offering quality shoes at way lower prices. The market shift was devastating to Dexter. In the blink of an eye, it effectively went to zero.

Had Buffett bought the company in cash, it would have been a very expensive mistake, but one that the company could have moved on from in short order. But since he used shares, the company didn't lose just the shares but also all the valuation growth those shares would have gained over time—a loss that hurt the company *and* every last shareholder.

There are plenty of people who would have blamed, made excuses, or outright lied about such an embarrassing and cataclysmic error. Others, so ashamed about the decision, might have broken under the weight and given up on the field entirely. But not Buffett. He owned up—publicly, repeatedly, and as a matter of practice.

In each annual shareholder letter, he allotted space for a kind of confessional. He would detail his biggest missteps from the year and, when relevant to a given moment, reflect on past miscalculations. As he said in his 2007 letter, he was going to continue to make mistakes. He might be one of the shrewdest investors the world has ever seen, but

CULTURE: BUILDING AN ECOSYSTEM OF EXCELLENCE

he's still human. And no one, no matter how extraordinary, will get it right all the time.

Buffett understood that buying into his own hype—believing he was some sort of finance god—would only set him up for bigger and more catastrophic falls when he inevitably messed up. To avoid the trap, he chose accountability, owning up to his errors as soon as he made them to foster trust and confidence in his company. By confessing to blunders, he was effectively saying to his shareholders: *We're going to get it wrong now and then. But we're going to tell you immediately when we do. We're going to learn, and we won't make the same mistake twice. We are responsible, trustworthy stewards of your hard-earned money. We're grateful for your investment in us, and we're going to show it by being transparent.*

His candor served two other goals. He knew that his annual letters were read not just by his shareholders but also people across the world who hoped to learn from him. In the internet age, Buffett's letters go viral every year. In revealing his missteps, he embodies the truism that we rarely learn from our successes, but we can always learn from our failures. In his openness, he hoped others could avoid the costly misjudgments he had already made.

Most importantly, Buffett was nurturing a culture of ownership and accountability—with the goal of continual improvement in pursuit of excellence. If the boss was always candid, then everyone across the company could be, too. His confessionals not only permitted and encouraged everyone across Berkshire Hathaway to own their successes *and* failures, but they reinforced that doing so was the expectation. When leaders exhibit the patterns of top performance every day, it makes it much harder for everyone else not to do the same.

You now have everything you need to live the ethos of top performance. Building habits around the patterns of performance takes time, but spotting the pitfalls is half the battle. You can't practice a pattern until you first recognize how you crumble in the face of challenge or fear. But you know this now. This means you're firmly on the path to achieving what matters most to you. This alone will change your life.

But what if you also need to change a team? What if you need to get your department, your students, your children, or any group of people who must perform at the top of their game oriented toward excellence?

When I coach leaders, the most common question I get is how to build a culture that elicits peak performance. Most find it intimidating, even impossible. Culture work often frustrates them more than anything else and can make them doubt their own capacity to lead.

Here's the good news: Creating a positive culture isn't rocket science. There is a science to it—but a simple one. Any leader willing to do the hidden work of performance can do it.

The Five Steps to Creating a Culture of Top Performance

Step 1: Personify Peak Performance

This is the hardest step, the heaviest lift. But guess what? You're already doing it. Just by showing up here with the desire to improve your own performance, you've fought half the battle. Because culture always begins with you.

Leaders set the tone of the culture in which they lead. Berkshire Hathaway might have posters listing their corporate values on every wall. Maybe one says "ownership." But if leaders don't back up those values with behaviors they exhibit daily, they're meaningless. Over time, hollow values breed cynicism, and cynicism rots culture.

The only cure for a toxic culture is leaders who practice what they preach. As a leader, culture starts with you. You hold the cards. If

CULTURE: BUILDING AN ECOSYSTEM OF EXCELLENCE

you blame, excuse, deceive, or quit, you're giving your team permission to do the same.

If you want a culture of ownership, a solution orientation, self-confrontation, and grit, then build these patterns into your daily actions.

> Don't just speak the language of performance— *show* it.

Don't just speak the language of performance—*show* it. Let your team see you model excellence every chance you get.

Another way to explain this step: Make the hidden work visible. Make it undeniable, aspirational, even inspirational.

Step 2: Set the Standard

And another way to explain this step? Make the hidden work explicit.

Teachers often tell me they struggle to make expectations clear to students. This reveals to me how daunting creating a culture of high expectations can feel—so daunting we sometimes miss the obvious, even when it's right in front of us. I don't say this with judgment. I say it with compassion. We've put leadership on such a high pedestal that it feels out of reach. That myth doesn't help anyone. It can paralyze people in leadership roles. What's worse, it's simply not true.

If you're reading this, you're already leading, at least in your own life. You care about achievement and are ready to meet high expectations for yourself. Leading others asks that you add this next step: Articulate the expectations you have of your team *to them*. Now you're a leader. And by following all these steps, you'll be a great leader who leads a thriving culture of achievement.

Spell out, with specificity, your standards for success and what top performance looks like. What goals are you and your team striving to meet? What daily behaviors go beyond talk and show real commitment?

Name them. Write them down. Post them. Document them. Repeat them constantly. Habits start with mindsets, and mindsets are made by default *or* design. Choose design.

Shared expectations are vital to a culture of achievement. Sometimes they need to be specific to a team and the work in front of you. But if you're at a loss as to where to begin, use the concepts of this book: Let the four pitfalls you commit to avoid and the four patterns you choose instead be your team's expectations. They work in any setting. And, in time, you can personalize them to your team.

Step 3: Challenge, and Be Challenged

Most leaders know they must hold their teams accountable if they want to meet ambitious goals. This is true—but it's only half the picture. I find that many leaders often forget that if accountability doesn't go both ways, then a culture of top performance will remain out of reach. Excellence demands accountability from everywhere and everyone, no matter one's age, experience level, title, or tenure.

The greater the gap in age, experience, or authority, the harder it can be for leaders to accept accountability from those junior to them. But the best leaders invite and accept accountability from everyone. To create these conditions, we leaders must do three things.

First: Make it clear that everyone on the team is expected to hold everyone else to account for shared values, behaviors, and expectations. Doing so will be uncomfortable to many people at first, so keep reminding them. When I'm in the gym with my players, it's appropriate and encouraged for them to hold me to account. But if you work in a large company, it likely doesn't make sense for an entry-level employee to directly hold a VP to account. In such cases, create appropriate pathways for feedback to cascade in all directions.

Second: Define and agree on the language everyone will use to hold each other accountable. If leaders are cruel or unclear in how they remind people they're not performing at their best, then this is not a culture of top performance. If junior people are disrespectful or hesitant in how they remind their leaders they're not embodying a pattern, then this is not a culture of top performance. Discuss as a team the gentle but direct and firm ways everyone will speak to each other when they see someone go into pitfall mode. Agree on the language used and actions taken to support each other in applying the patterns.

> A common language makes accountability conversations routine instead of anxious.

Write down this language. Post it in clear view. Reference it often. The more you use it, the less awkward it feels. A common language makes accountability conversations routine instead of anxious. When you see your team—yourself included—readily holding each other to account without emotion or fear, you'll know you have a healthy, thriving culture.

Third: Distill this shared language into a motto.

Step 4: Define Your Motto

Accountability language is key for tough conversations. A motto is a short expression that captures a guiding principle and can, by contrast, be sprinkled into daily talk—as a friendly nudge toward better performance or a way to head off a pitfall before it takes root.

Remember in the introduction, when Rocco caught me fudging my reps and not exactly owning it? To signal to him that I knew I wasn't living up to the expectations of our weightroom, I said, "The little reveals the lot." That's our team's motto. We all use it consistently in the gym. We say it at the start of a workout to get in the right mindset. We use it throughout to motivate each other. We use it to reinforce accountability. We say it at the end of a workout, to remind us to take pride in the hard work we just completed—because the little things matter. They add up to a lot. Our

> "The little reveals the lot."

motto is a quick reminder that we have high expectations for each other, and we believe we can meet them.

Mottos are a powerful cultural tool. They're a kind of rallying cry. They can motivate before, during, and after it's time to go into top-performance mode.

The best mottos are short, memorable, and positive. They're not criticisms or cutting. They're a shared idea the team has already agreed to. This way, a motto will not make anyone feel judged or defensive. It simply says: *Hey, remember that performance ethos you committed to? Now's the time. You've got this.*

Mottos are most effective when they resonate with everyone. Create one together so everyone in the group feels connected to it. And have fun with it. Whatever you choose, make sure it reflects the values and behaviors you've all committed to practice.

Step 5: Start on Day One—No Matter What Day It Is

Once you've digested these steps, act on them—starting day one. Day one might be the first day you assume a leadership position. Or it might be today. Either way, it's never too late to turn a culture of mediocrity into one of excellence.

Culture is a tricky thing: It can turn toxic in a day, but it takes time to cultivate a positive one. But you cannot create a healthy culture without consciously starting. As you set out to build the culture you want, don't come in like a Mack truck and try to change everything at once—you'll only alarm people and push them away. Be thoughtful and deliberate. Start with conversations about what you and your team

CULTURE: BUILDING AN ECOSYSTEM OF EXCELLENCE

view as the values and behaviors of top performance. Hone in on shared expectations. Identify them together. Codify them into language. Come up with a motto. Move at an effective and committed pace. Just be sure to move. Stasis has never led to greatness.

———

Culture is a conscious choice—made again and again, day after day. It starts with you, and it can start today.

AFTERWORD

You Hold the Power

The Pitfalls Are Always There. But So Are the Patterns

Where do you sell out?

When I ask an audience to take the Wonderlic, I want people to observe where they break. I want them to notice which pitfall they kick into when they feel challenged, uncertain, or exposed. I already know everyone in the room is capable of great achievement when they apply themselves. I'm not asking them to prove this to me through the Wonderlic. Their score is of no interest to me—where they break is. Because we all break under pressure. Not all the time, but eventually and maybe often. It's simply human to do so.

That's why I've repeatedly anchored the four pitfalls of low performance in our ancient wiring and deep-rooted psychology: To destigmatize them. To make it unmistakably clear that every single one of us is designed to go into survival mode at the first sign of threat. And that's not a flaw—it's a gift. If we didn't have a neurological system built to keep us alive and hardwired to seek community and safety, we wouldn't have lasted long enough for achievement to matter.

But here's the thing: Our brilliant survival system worked so well that it helped us evolve to the point where survival isn't the primary concern anymore. Now we get to pursue meaning, mastery, purpose. We get to build lives that are about more than just getting through the day.

The problem is, as we now understand, that our wiring hasn't caught up. We still respond to a missed goal or difficult conversation as if it's a saber-toothed tiger.

Real threats do, of course, still exist. And when we confront them—hopefully with extreme rarity—thank goodness our system is on alert. But most of the time? It's misfiring. It's seeing danger where there's just discomfort. And that's the challenge of top performance—not rejecting the survival system but learning to live in concert with it. Learning to hear the alarm bells and ask, "Is this a real threat, or is this just my wiring getting it wrong?"

Here's the clue: If the alarm bell sends you into a pitfall, it's probably not a real threat. That's where the hidden work comes in—the awareness of all those inner reflexes, our self-defeating thought processes. All those habits of mind we must change first so that we can then change the outer work, our actual performance.

The first step to top performance is developing a practice of noticing your pitfalls. They're fast, automatic, and often subconscious—which means detection must be deliberate. You can't override what you don't recognize.

Most of us use all four pitfalls at different times. But in my experience coaching thousands of people, most default to the same one or two when the pressure hits.

So start with self-awareness. The next time you find yourself struggling to persist through something difficult, pause and ask:

- What kind of setback has put me into pitfall mode?
- Why does it feel unsafe? Am I actually unsafe?
- Which of the four pitfalls is activated right now?

Over time, you'll notice patterns. Certain types of challenges will show up again and again—and so will your reflexive response. But the more you understand what unnecessarily triggers your survival mechanism and which pitfalls you then tend to use, the less power they have to hijack you.

Eventually, you'll know which pitfalls are your go-to crutches. That's essential. You have to name them before you can conquer them. You have to know the trap to apply the right pattern to climb out of it.

And above all: Don't beat yourself up for falling into pitfall mode. It's not weakness. It's not failure. It's just ancient wiring doing its job.

This is where humor helps. This work is serious—but you don't have to take yourself too seriously. And, really, *should* you take your primitive brain too seriously? When you think about it, it can be quite comical.

A colleague gives you feedback, and your brain acts like you're being hunted. A client says "no," and you shame spiral like it's an indictment of your overall worthiness in life. You don't finish the workout, so you eat an entire pizza and call it balance.

We've all been there. And when you can laugh at it—when you can say, "There's my old wiring again"—you disarm it. You recognize the reflex, override it, and step back into the pattern.

That's what this work is. Not perfection. Not posturing. Not pretending you're above it all. Just self-awareness, deliberate practice, and progress.

> That's what this work is. Not perfection. Not posturing. Not pretending you're above it all. Just self-awareness, deliberate practice, and progress.

Because the best performers aren't perfect. Not even close. They're just consistent. And that consistency doesn't come from being better than everyone else. It comes from knowing themselves better and believing their wiring a little less.

Now go get after it. I know you can.

References

Chapter 2

1. Greenberg, Jeff, Tom Pyszczynski, and Sheldon Solomon, "The Causes and Consequences of a Need for Self-Esteem: A Terror Management Theory," in *Public Self and Private Self*, ed. Roy F. Baumeister (New York: Springer, 1986), 189–212, https://doi.org/10.1007/978-1-4613-9564-5_10.
2. Tavris, Carol and Elliot Aronson, *Mistakes Were Made (but Not by Me): Why We Justify Foolish Beliefs, Bad Decisions, and Hurtful Acts*, 3rd ed. (New York: Mariner Books, 2020).
3. Baumeister, Roy F. and Dianne M. Tice, "Self-esteem and Responses to Success and Failure: Subsequent Performance and Intrinsic Motivation," *Journal of Personality* 53, no. 3 (1985): 450–67, https://doi.org/10.1111/j.1467-6494.1985.tb00376.x.
4. *The Pivot Podcast*, "Mike Tomlin on Pitt Legacy, Super Bowls, Flores Hiring & Future without Big Ben," season 1, episode 47, hosted by Fred Taylor, Channing Crowder, and Ryan Clark, aired June 21, 2022, on YouTube, 1:05:24, https://www.youtube.com/watch?v=HsJ2Pq8L1-M.
5. *Tampa Bay Times*, "Serena Williams' Grand Slam Bid Ends with Stunning Loss in U.S. Open Semifinal," published September 12, 2015, https://www.tampabay.com/sports/tennis/serena-williams-loses-grand-slam-bid-in-us-open-semifinal/2245156/.
6. Rotter, Julian B. "Generalized Expectancies for Internal versus External Control of Reinforcement". *Psychological Monographs: General and Applied* 80, no. 1 (1966). https://doi.org/10.1037/h0092976.

7. Canal, Emily. "First, I Lost on 'Shark Tank.' Then, I Sold My Startup for Over $1 Billion& *Inc.*, July/August 2018 issue, published June 27, 2018. https://www.inc.com/magazine/201808/emily-canal/how-i-did-it-jamie-siminoff-ring.html.

Chapter 3

1. U.S. Census Bureau, *American Community Survey 5-Year Estimates*, 2023, Census Reporter Profile page for Coalinga-Huron Unified School District, CA, http://censusreporter.org/profiles/97000US0609120-coalinga-huron-unified-school-district-ca/.
2. Roosevelt, Theodore. 1910. "Citizenship in a Republic& Speech delivered at the Sorbonne, Paris, April 23. Reproduced in *The American Presidency Project*, ed. Gerhard Peters and John T. Woolley. Accessed May 28, 2025. https://theodoreroosevelt.org/content.aspx?page_id=22&club_id=991271&module_id=339364.
3. Brown, Brené. *Daring Greatly: How the Courage to Be Vulnerable Transforms the Way We Live, Love, Parent, and Lead.* New York: Gotham Books, 2012.
4. Festinger, Leon. *A Theory of Cognitive Dissonance.* Stanford, CA: Stanford University Press, 1957.
5. Berglas, Steven and Edward E. Jones, "Drug Choice as a Self-Handicapping Strategy in Response to Noncontingent Success," *Journal of Personality and Social Psychology* 36, no. 4 (1978): 405–417, https://doi.org/10.1037/0022-3514.36.4.405.
6. Csikszentmihalyi, Mihaly. *Flow: The Psychology of Optimal Experience.* New York: Harper & Row, 1990.
7. Hamilton, Bethany, "Limitations Aren't Excuses," *Bethany Hamilton Blog*, August 20, 2020, https://bethanyhamilton.com/blog/limitations-arent-excuses.

REFERENCES

Chapter 4

1. Brooks, Michael L. and William B. Swann Jr., "The Evolution and Psychology of Self-Deception," *Behavioral and Brain Sciences* 34, no. 1 (2011): 1–56, https://doi.org/10.1017/S0140525X10001354.
2. Ibid.
3. Nobel, Carmen, "Reflecting on Work Improves Job Performance," *HBS Working Knowledge*, May 5, 2014, https://www.library.hbs.edu/working-knowledge/reflecting-on-work-improves-job-performance.
4. Duval, Shelley, and Robert A. Wicklund. *A Theory of Objective Self-Awareness*. New York: Academic Press, 1972.
5. Lyddon, William J., David R. Yowell, and Hubert J. M. Hermans. 2006. "The Self-Confrontation Method: Theory, Research, and Practical Utility& Counselling Psychology Quarterly 19 (1): 27–43. https://doi.org/10.1080/09515070600589719.

Chapter 5

1. Shenhav, Amitai, Matthew M. Botvinick, and Jonathan D. Cohen, "The Expected Value of Control: An Integrative Theory of Anterior Cingulate Cortex Function," *Neuron* 79, no. 2 (2013): 217–240, https://doi.org/10.1016/j.neuron.2013.07.007.
2. Segal, Gillian Zoe, "How Billionaire Sara Blakely Refused to Let Rejection Stop Her," *The Story Exchange*, April 29, 2015, https://thestoryexchange.org/sara-blakely-refused-fear-failure-stop/.
3. Frank, Robert, "Billionaire Sara Blakely Says Secret to Success Is Failure," *CNBC Make It*, October 16, 2013, https://www.cnbc.com/2013/10/16/billionaire-sara-blakely-says-secret-to-success-is-failure.html.
4. Duckworth, Angela, "Q&A," *Angela Duckworth*, accessed July 25, 2025, https://angeladuckworth.com/qa/.
5. Berger, Michele W., "What Factors Predict Success? New Research from Angela Duckworth and Colleagues Finds That Characteristics beyond Intelligence Influence Long-Term Achievement," *Penn Today*, November

4, 2019, University of Pennsylvania, https://penntoday.upenn.edu/news/Penn-Angela-Duckworth-looks-beyond-grit-predict-success.
6. Dweck, Carol S. *Mindset: The New Psychology of Success*. New York: Random House, 2006.
7. Bandura, Albert. "Self-Efficacy: Toward a Unifying Theory of Behavioral Change& *Psychological Review* 84, no. 2 (1977): 191–215. https://doi.org/10.1037/0033-295X.84.2.191.
8. Duckworth, Angela, *Grit: The Power of Passion and Perseverance* (New York: Scribner, 2016).
9. Cunningham, Lillian, "Misty Copeland's Perseverance," *On Leadership*, *The Washington Post*, April 10, 2015, https://www.washingtonpost.com/news/on-leadership/wp/2015/04/10/misty-copelands-perseverance/.
10. Copeland, Misty, *Ballerina Body: Dancing and Eating Your Way to a Leaner, Stronger, and More Graceful You* (New York: Grand Central Publishing, 2017).
11. Hartman, Steve, "Teen Who Walked Six Miles to 8th Grade Graduation Gets College Scholarship on the Spot," CBS News, June 23, 2023, https://www.cbsnews.com/news/teen-walked-6-miles-8th-grade-graduation-college-scholarship/.

Chapter 6

1. Buffett, Warren E. 2007 Berkshire Hathaway Inc. Annual Shareholder Letter. Omaha, NE: Berkshire Hathaway Inc., February 29, 2008. https://www.berkshirehathaway.com/letters/2007ltr.pdf.

Acknowledgments

Every book is a team effort, and this one is no exception. *The Hidden Work* could not have come to life without the extraordinary people who poured their time, talent, and belief into it.

To Kelly Griego—thank you for being the hidden gem behind *The Hidden Work*. Your presence, guidance, and encouragement remind me that what often goes unseen is what shines the brightest.

To Kheila Casas—your remarkable artistry gave this book its face. The cover is more than design; it's a symbol, a story in itself. You didn't just capture the spirit of this work—you elevated it.

To Jimmy Casas—friend, mentor, and the best publishing partner I could ever ask for. Thank you for walking this road with me, for challenging me, for believing in me, and for modeling the very ethos this book is about.

To Jeff Zoul—your edits were more than corrections; they were refinements that helped this work breathe more deeply. Thank you for sharpening my words without dulling their soul.

And to my family, colleagues, readers, and every person who does their own hidden work—you are the reason I write.

About the Author

Weston Kieschnick is a globally recognized speaker, best-selling author, and one of today's leading voices on performance, leadership, and culture. An award-winning educator and TEDx speaker, Weston has advised leaders in every U.S. state and more than thirty countries, helping organizations build cultures where people thrive. His books and acclaimed podcast have inspired millions. Known for blending grit, humor, and hard-won expertise, Weston equips leaders to create extraordinary results in schools, teams, and organizations everywhere. Connect with Weston: westonkieschnick.com and westonkieschnick@gmail.com

More from ConnectEDD Publishing

Since 2015, ConnectEDD has worked to transform education by empowering educators to become better-equipped to teach, learn, and lead. What started as a small company designed to provide professional learning events for educators has grown to include a variety of services to help educators and administrators address essential challenges. ConnectEDD offers instructional and leadership coaching, professional development workshops focusing on a variety of educational topics, a roster of nationally recognized educator associates who possess hands-on knowledge and experience, educational conferences custom-designed to meet the specific needs of schools, districts, and state/national organizations, and ongoing, personalized support, both virtually and onsite. In 2020, ConnectEDD expanded to include publishing services designed to provide busy educators with books and resources consisting of practical information on a wide variety of teaching, learning, and leadership topics. Please visit us online at connecteddpublishing.com or contact us at: info@connecteddpublishing.com

Recent Publications:

Live Your Excellence: Action Guide by Jimmy Casas

Culturize: Action Guide by Jimmy Casas

Daily Inspiration for Educators: Positive Thoughts for Every Day of the Year by Jimmy Casas

Eyes on Culture: Multiply Excellence in Your School by Emily Paschall

Pause. Breathe. Flourish. Living Your Best Life as an Educator by William D. Parker

L.E.A.R.N.E.R. Finding the True, Good, and Beautiful in Education by Marita Diffenbaugh

Educator Reflection Tips Volume II: Refining Our Practice by Jami Fowler-White

Handle With Care: Managing Difficult Situations in Schools with Dignity and Respect by Jimmy Casas and Joy Kelly

Disruptive Thinking: Preparing Learners for Their Future by Eric Sheninger

Permission to be Great: Increasing Engagement in Your School by Dan Butler

Daily Inspiration for Educators: Positive Thoughts for Every Day of the Year, Volume II by Jimmy Casas

The 6 Literacy Levers: Creating a Community of Readers by Brad Gustafson

The Educator's ATLAS: Your Roadmap to Engagement by Weston Kieschnick

In This Season: Words for the Heart by Todd Nesloney, LaNesha Tabb, Tanner Olson, and Alice Lee

MORE FROM CONNECTEDD PUBLISHING

Leading with a Humble Heart: A 40-Day Devotional for Leaders by Zac Bauermaster

Recalibrate the Culture: Our Why…Our Work…Our Values by Jimmy Casas

Creating Curious Classrooms: The Beauty of Questions by Emma Chiappetta

Crafting the Culture: 45 Reflections on What Matters Most by Joe Sanfelippo and Jeffrey Zoul

Improving School Mental Health: The Thriving School Community Solution by Charle Peck and Dr. Cameron Caswell

Building Authenticity: A Blueprint for the Leader Inside You by Todd Nesloney and Tyler Cook

Connecting Through Conversation: A Playbook for Talking with Kids by Erika Bare and Tiffany Burns

The Dream Factory: Designing a Purposeful Life by Mark Trumbo

Stories Behind Stances: Creating Empathy Through Hearing "The Other Side" by Chris Singleton

Happy Eyes: Becoming All Things to All People by Ryan Tillman

The Generative Age: Artificial Intelligence and the Future of Education by Alana Winnick

Recalibrate the Culture: Action Guide by Jimmy Casas

Leading with PEOPLE: A Six Pillar Framework for Fruitful Leadership by Zac Bauermaster

A School Leader's Guide to Reclaiming Purpose by Frederick C. Buskey

Foundations of an Elite Culture: Building Success with High Standards and a Positive Environment by David Arencibia

Personalize: Meeting the Needs of All Learners by Eric Sheninger and Nicki Slaugh

The Five Principles of Educator Professionalism: Rebuilding Trust in Schools by Nason Lollar

Words on the Wall: Culturizing Your Classroom For Observable Impact by Jimmy Casas and Cale Birk

School of Engagement: 45 Activities to Ignite Student Learning by Jonathan Alsheimer

Intentional Instructional Moves: Strategic Steps to Accelerate Student Learning by Sherry St. Clair

Overcoming Education: Complex Challenges, Difficult People, and the Art of Making a Difference by Brad R. Gustafson

The Language of Behavior: A Framework to Elevate Student Success by Charle Peck and Joshua Stamper

Whose Permission Are You Waiting For? An Educator's Guide to Doing What You Love by William D. Parker

The Leader You're Not…And Why It's Just As Important As the Leader You Are by Scott Borba

The Growth-Minded Leader by Tyler Cook

Day by Day: 180 Days of Hope and Encouragement by Zac Bauermaster

Make Your Move: For Ambitious People Ready to Live Their Aspirations by Marlon Styles, Jr.

www.ingramcontent.com/pod-product-compliance
Lightning Source LLC
Chambersburg PA
CBHW060526030426
42337CB00015B/1995